sto

The
People
Are
the
Church

The
People
Are
the
Church

Eugene C. Kennedy, M.M.

Doubleday & Company, Inc., Garden City, New York
1969

Library of Congress Catalog Card Number 75–86889
Copyright © 1969 by Eugene C. Kennedy
All Rights Reserved
Printed in the United States of America
First Edition

Remember not the former things, nor consider the things of old. Behold, I am doing a new thing: now it springs forth, do you not perceive it?

Isaiah 43:18,19

Christ instituted this new covenant, that is to say,
the new testament, in His blood, by calling together
a people made up of Jew and Gentile, making them one,
not according to the flesh but in the spirit.
This was to be the new People of God.

Dogmatic Constitution on the Church, par. 9

Contents

Introduction

I am writing this book because I believe in the Gospels and their injunction about being clear when we speak our "yea" or "nay." It has been my hope in writing to translate the meaning of events or personal experiences so that people could better understand them, especially in regard to the Christian life of the People of God. I hope that this book will continue to mediate some of the Christian experience of our times. But I hope that it will do more than that.

Understanding is a powerful and indispensable ingredient in psychotherapy. There are times, however, when the counselor must use his skills to penetrate the defenses of his patient. Respectfully rather than vindictively, he must, if any progress is to be made, confront the other with the meaning of his behavior. It is my hope that this book will contain the elements of confrontation, not to express personal anger or frustration, but to stimulate and promote growth in all of us who together constitute the Church. Defenses exist which must be penetrated if the Church is to continue successfully in the

search for self-understanding that began so magnificently in the Second Vatican Council.

The Church is in so many ways comparable to a person
struggling to understand himself in therapy. There are
times when he gets angry and feels keenly the tension of
the divisions within himself. He can be disgusted and
tempted to let the whole process go and to carry on in the
pain of half growth. It is when someone is willing to
struggle with him that he gets the courage to move forward in the pursuit of self-knowledge and fuller growth.
The therapist must believe in him but he must also be
ready to face him with the facts of reality.

This is an age in which we must continue to have faith
in the Church because we know that the Spirit is available
to give it the fullness of life. To receive the Spirit, it must
open itself fully. This, however, involves laying aside
defenses and distorted self-understandings which are no
longer useful. Those who love the Church must now be
strong enough to confront it, not to condemn it, but to
challenge it, even in its discouragement and anguish, to
move forward. There is a lot of wisdom in Hudson In-
stitute director Herman Kahn's remark that "you never
get the people to understand what's confusing unless you
make it stark." Confrontation of the facts requires an unblinking look at them in their stark reality. It is because
we have faith in the Church as People of God that we
can challenge our own defenses. It is faith in the promises
of the Spirit that gives us the courage to do this. This is
the faith that makes us whole.

I am writing this book because so many people within
the Church are suffering and because there seems to be a
danger that the Church will get discouraged in its efforts
to renew itself. It is this discouragement, which results in
a rejection of the tasks of aggiornamento, that allows the

Church to settle for an uneasy compromise rather than full growth. This is the source of much suffering for members of the Church who are earnestly committed to its mission of bringing salvation to man. Many of these are priests and religious but there are even greater numbers of laity who yearn to serve the world through the instrumentality of the Church. These are the people for whom compromise in renewal is crushing.

There has been so much hesitation and caution, so much reliance on worn-out phrases about making haste slowly, so much defensiveness that these people have come to wonder whether Church leadership is seriously interested in giving itself fully to the world. This is particularly true regarding the essential task of institutional reform. Slight modifications, somewhat like automobile styling changes which leave the basic design untouched, seem all that are tolerable. Yet the signs of the time are abundantly clear about the need for institutional renewal. It is difficult to believe that people cannot read them. Those who refuse to read them are either defensively looking the other way or they are playing the game, with a fine Latin hand showing, in the tradition of the curial minds who have survived the various rages and storms of history and who mistakenly think that they have triumphed serenely over all of them.

Typical of the hundreds of letters I have received is this excerpt from a teaching sister who finds her energies sapped because of the slowness of the pace of positive change in the Church:

Father, there are many of us overwhelmed and discouraged, fighting a double battle with little strength, less hope and no moral support. Our name is legion. We sense what must be done but often courage and conviction are lacking.

The servants of the Church who suffer because of the temporizing and uncertain movements of its leadership are indeed legion. The laity suffer as well, not just because of the current confusion over birth control and Church authority, but because they are yearning for something from the Church that will enrich their lives and give them a vision and a faith by which they can live and which they can draw on in the task of raising their families. The Church, as servant, owes this to them, and it owes it to them now.

For the sake of all these people, we are the generation with the responsibility of becoming new, according to the perennial vocation of the Church. This obviously involves building on the authentic growth of the past. The important point is that we achieve something of the future that we can share with others right now. As the People of God we have a covenant with each other to pursue the same goals and to share our faith and love with all mankind. It is such understanding of our corporate mission that must motivate us to renew the institutional forms of the Church. The question centers on institutional integrity. Do the institutions of the Church contribute to its carrying out its mandate of service as effectively as possible? Those which do not must be repatterned so that they may become a true instrumentation of service.

It is time to take a stand for man. This is the Church's main business. The Church is for man, and it must meet his needs or it is operating from a basic misunderstanding of itself. It is so easy for any large institution to transfer most of its energies into institutional survival and thereby to obscure its fundamental purpose. This is a problem that has been faced by hospitals and universities, by the courts and by the professions. The great and present temptation of the institutional Church is to remain defensive, to go at renewal in a halting way, in hopes that the forms will survive even if the main function is not carried out.

I write this with great sympathy for bishops and superiors who now exercise responsible authority within the Church. Few of them are ambitious, although some of them are career-conscious enough to allow their own visions of promotion to guide their measured participation in the activity of the Church. They are the ones with a problem, as I see it. These are the uncertain men who are ruled by fear that something dear to them in position or promotion will be lost if they truly commit themselves to the task of renewing the Church.

One of psychologist Carl Rogers' most stimulating observations concerns the defenses we can all set up against really listening to other people. He points out that if we really listen to another, we might change, and change threatens our comfortable ideas about ourselves. This is exactly the kind of problem some people in positions of leadership have. They listen quite selectively to the Christian community and are extremely skilled at filtering out anything that might challenge them to change themselves. That they fail to understand the need to change themselves and that they cannot hear the voices that cry out for it merely illustrates the depth of the personal problem, the origin and solution of which are their responsibility.

There are many people in positions of leadership whose problems arise from within themselves. It is not always a discordant and critical laity or a restless clergy that constitutes the source of their difficulties. They have problems because they do not read the signs of the

times, because they do not trust people, and because
they do not open themselves to the Spirit. They resist
the impulses to constructive change and they do not
realize how late the hour already is. They have allowed
opportunities for building the Church in this world to
go by because they do not, at times, recognize the potential function of the Church in serving the world. These
people have the problem because they have not listened
enough to the experience of the Christian community.
When they choose to make decisions out of relationship
to it, they are surprised when their people respond in
disagreement. They can then spectacularly misinterpret
this as an attack on their authority. This is the logic of
the Italian cardinal so sure of his divine pipeline that he
said recently, "In governing the diocese, I cannot let
myself be guided by the people. I must follow God. Only
the bishop can judge the needs of his people" (*New York
Times*, December 11, 1968). The point is, does he?

Perhaps the people can judge their own needs fairly
well. It is to respond to their needs that Christ established
the Church. I hope and pray that some authorities in the
Church will realize that they themselves can and do
possess major problems which interfere with Church
functioning. They must deal with their own problems and
not expect the people to solve them by turning away as
meek and chastened sheep. There is a meaning in the
dissenting responses of the laity to the statements of
various churchmen. If the latter sense it correctly, they
may yet understand how the Spirit can speak through
all of God's people.

The worst problem that most of these leaders have is
their estrangement or isolation from the Christian community. Living at a distance from it, accepting the inter-
pretation of aides as fact, it is no surprise that they are

sometimes insensitive to the action of the Spirit in their
flocks. I emphasize the proper attribution of the problem
to isolated leaders to encourage the many good people
who have begun to doubt themselves in the face of such
little response from above them. They are right and the
Church has much to learn from them.

There are, of course, genuinely open and sensitive
Church leaders whose presence is a grace for us all. They
need some encouragement too, inasmuch as they can be
men made lonely by their own deep knowledge of the
needs of the Church and the mountainous obstacles that
prevent the Church from acting more bravely and consistently. I think, then, that we must confront our lack
of faith, both in the Spirit and in God's people. I do not
exempt myself or the reader from the need to face ourselves honestly about our role in renewal.

It was David Hume, I believe, who noted that the
corruptions of Christianity were superstition and enthusiasm. The first of these is typically High Church, where
doctrine that is not considered capable of development
hardens into a kind of dogma which ends up as rigid
superstition. The second is Low Church, in which doctrine
is distasteful from the start and where it can disappear
altogether in the raptures of the Spirit. These are the
temptations to corruption that are present today in the
Church. They must be confronted because they are both
excesses and distortions of the Christian life. Both are
presently enjoying a field day, mostly at the expense of
the healthy members of the Church who constitute its
real strength. These latter are the ones who are suffering
most at this time. It is to their hopes that we must
respond with renewal that is substantial and prompt.
Failing to do this, we merely leave the business of renewal to the extremists, the compulsive introverts or the

impulsive extroverts. Neither of these understands or can respond to the ordinary religious needs of human beings.

It is for ordinary human beings, made quite extraordinary by God's action on them, that this book is written. They are the salt of the earth if ever this commodity is to be found. They are trustworthy and they deserve the best the Church can give them in their efforts to lead good and loving lives. They are largely forgotten in the dramatic news events of renewal. But they are what the Church is for and it is time that we took them more seriously.

Eugene C. Kennedy

Glen Ellyn, Ill.
Grand Beach, Mich.
F. S.

Where Seldom Is Heard
an Encouraging Word

The Catholic landscape resembles more a pitted and smoking no man's land than it does the city of God. The hard-line fundamentalist tone pervades the times. While the long-range prospects for the success of massive retaliation on the part of authoritarianism are slight, its present resurgence is quite remarkable in its evangelical fervor. The presses have been running hot with warnings, condemnations, and assorted cautions about alleged deviations and excesses in renewal. All the machinery of discreet inquiry and secret hearings has been oiled up and set, sparks jumping from its long unused flywheels, into motion again. Is this any way to run a Church? It is indeed difficult to think so.

From the classic ecclesiastical pippin's eagerness to proclaim Jacqueline Onassis a public sinner to the campaigns urging Catholics to sign loyalty oaths to the Pope, the forces of righteousness are on the offensive. Dialogue has never been their dish and so they find the era of condemnations especially heartening. Unable to wither hands or to blight orchards, they content themselves with quenching the smoking flax of thought wherever this is possible. They have made their own the words of Billy Sunday, "I have no interest in a God who does not smite."

Nothing has ever failed quite so magnificently for the Church as the tactics of suppression. Burning men or their books has never put an end to their ideas. "The paper burns," as Rabbi Akiba ben Joseph said at the stake when he and the Torah were being burned, "but the words fly away." While the torch has not yet been set to modern-day Catholic thinkers who are struggling to understand their faith more deeply, the atmosphere has been made exceedingly warm and unpleasant for them. The lessons of the past failures of such oppressive tactics have apparently not discouraged the heresy hunters of the present. There has been little effort to meet and deal maturely with the Christian community in its struggle to deepen its convictions about the essential meaning of the Gospels.

The notion, much less the spirit, of encouragement is practically nonexistent at the present time in the Church. Encouragement, however, is a traditional kind of Christian virtue. It means, literally, to put courage into another. This is surely the task of those who bear the responsibility of authority within the Church. Yet one must grope through a thicket of cautions in order to find a few words that are hopeful or encouraging to those sincere Christians who have committed themselves to the authentic spirit of renewal.

Paul's epistles fairly abound with encouragement for his Christian communities. Paul, as we know, was no stranger to the art of confrontation, having "bearded" the then Holy Father Peter, "to his face," in one of our earliest examples of lively dialogue in the infant Church.

The pastoral documents of today do have sections which are marked with a flavor of deserved compassion for the sinner. This is all to the good; but they contain little that puts courage into the people struggling to lead good lives. There is, contrary to the suppositions of authoritarianism, no lack of saintliness in the contemporary Church. These are the Christians who need encouragement if they are to share their faith and good works with the world around them. One gets the feeling that the authors of many modern ecclesial documents have been living in ivory towers rather than in listening posts on the human condition.

The medium is unfortunately all too accurately the message. It is one of restriction rather than the enlargement of human experience, of closing people off rather than of opening them up so that they can respond to the action of the Holy Spirit. Dissent is still regarded as highly suspect. It must be sweetened and diluted so that it is a flavorless kind of gruel which, while not harmful in its effects, fails as a source of nourishment. Dissent becomes more difficult, even by those who would carry it out in a respectful and constructive way. They have come to understand the worldly wisdom of E. B. White's observation that "to disagree with anybody or anything is to run the risk of taking oneself out of the money."

It is not only theologians and other thinkers and writers who have experienced the lack of encouragement for their work. It is true for the great rank and file of priests and religious who are constantly reminded that they must proceed with caution and control more than with enthusiasm and daring as they try to renew themselves. Indeed, one of the real scandals of Christendom is the savage kind of condemnation that many intelligent and progressive churchmen and churchwomen have had to

endure during this period. Not only encouragement but
also charity and understanding have been in short supply
as they try to develop more effective modes of responding
to the needs of God's people. Some of the more rigid
members of religious groups have been nothing less than
savage in their criticism and their active if subtle ostraciz-
ing of colleagues who have tried to think new thoughts
and work toward positive and constructive change. The
amount of frustration and suffering that has been visited
upon sisters, for example, who have done nothing more
than change their habits is bewildering indeed. I recall
being cornered by an older member of a woman's religious community recently who instructed me to get after
the younger members because of their devious ways.
"They are nothing but floozies," she said, "and it is time
to do something about them." Sincere women, who want
as much as Theresa of Ávila to be daughters of the
Church, have been accused of being bad women merely
because they have wanted to serve the community of the
Church more fully.

There is an uneasiness in the minds of many extremely
conservative and authoritarian leaders about something
the Church should surely understand well, the human
love that is proof that the Holy Spirit still works in this
world. They seem awkward in dealing with this phenomenon, almost embarrassed that Christians should be
tempted to love one another. One of the profound dis-
appointments of Pope Paul's encyclical *Humanae Vitae*
is its incomplete treatment of the nature of love. There is
indeed much to say about the sacrificial aspects of
human love. "Of Human Life" leaves most of this unsaid.
This is just what the Church should be able to speak of
with the depths of understanding that have come from
its experience with man over the centuries. Instead man

is reminded of his potentially evil character. At the same time, and in an almost angelic summons, he is called to an ideal for which his presumably warped nature would ill fit him. This is not to say that the Holy Father is wrong. It is merely to emphasize that he was more cautionary than encouraging to the vast numbers of men and women who look to him for some understanding of the major concern of their lives, that of loving one another truly and deeply. It takes courage to love in a world that so misunderstands it. Man is hardly helped if he is merely reminded again and again of the things he can do wrong. What he obviously needs, in addition to compassion for his sins, is an inspiriting of his person for the positive tasks of the Christian life.

Perhaps there is no aspect of human personality which deserves more positive orientation and encouragement than sexuality. It is more often treated under the old title of "evil under the belt" than as the genuinely human and all-pervading dimension of life which it truly is. In a world strewn with errant and distorted understandings of sex, it might be helpful if the Church were able to offer more encouragement to those who are striving to put sexuality into its deserved Christian perspective. Yet nothing stirs the bile of the righteous more than this subject. Nothing betrays the puritanical and uneducated mind more than a zestful crusade against supposedly rampant lust. But lust is not rampant among conscientious Christians who merely want to love one another more maturely and to understand their own sexuality as a part of this. In no area where man seeks to find himself does he need encouragement rather than condemnation more than in the understanding of his sexuality. The best way to accomplish this is to encourage the full development of the human person. This is impossible when people are fixated on treating him as a blind and stumbling beast perennially oriented to sexual excess.

If some churchmen have been discouraging about human sexuality, there are many more who feel that the real issue is obedience. Prudence is vaguely and awkwardly invoked to dampen the enthusiasm of the young and the energetic, on whose shoulders the burdens of the future Church already rest. It is dangerous, however, to interpret every new thought or insight as a challenge to the authority of the Church. This is almost a habit of mind with certain ecclesiastics whose commitment is obviously to preserve an institutional framework rather than to free people so that they may lead the resurrected life in Christ which is the essence of Christianity.

This type of ecclesiastic has a great fear of losing control over people. For him, renewal is acceptable only if it represents the semblance rather than the substance of change. Cross the line that he draws, however, even in quite accidental aspects of the exercise of freedom, and he reacts as if the whole authority of the Church were suddenly placed in danger. This demonstrates more his own lack of confidence in himself and his authority than it does any surge of disobedience among the faithful.

The basic problem with some of those in places of power is their mistrust of human beings. They apparently believe that unless man is kept constantly under surveillance and control everything they hold dear is in jeopardy. What makes them anxious, obviously, is when free men choose to act freely. While this is the highest expression of human promise and dignity, it disconcerts the powerful for a very simple reason: it takes some aspect of the lives of others out of their control. When things are not completely in their control, they get anxious. Because they do not enjoy being anxious, they move to restrict freedom in others. Contingency has no place in the lexicon of their Christianity. Conversely, their kind of Christianity has no place in the lexicon of the authentic Christian community.

They are so fearful that people may make mistakes and that they will be responsible for them, that they look on freedom as a highly volatile substance that should be doled out only in small portions. There is something strangely and inappropriately messianic in their perception of themselves when they are afraid to allow other people to be free. It takes courage to allow other people to be free, as parents everywhere can tell them. Nobody grows or reaches any kind of maturity unless they are trusted. Trust does not live long unless those who bestow it are willing to encourage others freely to do their best. As long as they are fearful that they will do their worst, they will not be able to help them to become truly grown-up Christians.

That is why there has been so little rational experimentation at the time when it is most needed in the Church. Experiments, by their very nature, are designed to find out what will happen when man alters the conditions of his life. No experiment can be carried on unless there is an openness to outcomes that cannot be fully predicted. This is exactly what makes certain authoritarian leaders upset. They will allow no experiments unless they can control the outcome. Since this is impossible, they tend to discourage experimentation in general.

There is evidence that the Christian community, to which Church leaders should listen more and preach less, is developing a greater maturity of religious practice. It seems clear that one of the reasons for the change in the practice of penance is that Christians have developed a new and internalized sense of responsibility in judging the goodness or sinfulness of their actions. This is a sign of growth in religious maturity and, because of it, the whole practice of confession within the Church is gradually reshaping itself. This kind of mature self-evaluation in the sight of God needs encouragement and yet few have praised Catholic people for their newfound and more selective use of the sacrament of Penance.

It is interesting, in light of this, to examine the characteristics of the religion of childhood. As listed by Gordon Allport, the late and distinguished psychologist, they are as follows:

The religion of childhood:

1. is accepted on authority.
2. is imitative of others.
3. is verbalistic and ritualistic.
4. is anthropomorphic.
5. is egocentric.
6. is non-reflective.
7. is spontaneous.
8. is wondering.

According to students of religious psychology the first six characteristics must transform themselves if an individual is to attain religious maturity. Religious belief must be internalized and flow from the individual. So too, it must reflect itself in the person's life more than just in religious practices. Mature religious behavior connotes a better understanding of God and an openness of the person to sharing life and love with others. Mature religious behavior is reflective in the sense of Ambrose's faith that seeks to understand itself. The last two characteristics, that religion be spontaneous and wondering, are values to be preserved in the adult if he is not to be the victim of highly stylized and deadening religious practice. All too often, in the non-encouraging atmosphere of today, there is an effort to reinforce the first six characteristics and to eliminate spontaneity and wonder. In other words, an authoritarian and overcontrolled atmosphere tends to preserve the immature characteristics of religion and people and to discourage the more vital qualities which should carry over into later life.

Christians are struggling for a more developed religious sense. They need large measures of encouragement to carry on this process. The prevailing winds blow strangely against them. It is a hazardous proposition to give people the freedom and trust they need in order to become adult Christians. Something of childhood will be lost. If Church leaders cannot endure this, then they misunderstand the task of their leadership. The Christian community is pursuing this ideal even without encouragement. It would be helpful if some Church leaders could recognize that this indeed is the process that is under way. They should rejoice at it rather than try to repress it.

One of the great threats of the era of non-encouragement is that it is anti-intellectual and therefore antihuman in its bent. The Church is for man—thinking, feeling man. It should make him fully man so that with all his powers he can respond to God's grace. Anti-intellectualism, one of the characteristics of the fundamentalist spirit, can only alienate further a generation of better educated and more serious Christians. It can only generate greater suffering in the scholars who have so recently emerged from what Monsignor John Tracy Ellis characterized only a dozen years ago as a basically "ghetto mentality." The Catholic intellectual community needs encouragement, not just toleration. It can only move away from an institutional Church that looks at it quite suspiciously and mistrustfully.

The other danger of the present atmosphere is that it destroys the position of moderates while, at the same time, it hardens the defenses of extremists. It has become progressively more difficult for moderates to maintain their hope for the healthy and orderly growth for which they have been working within the Church. They get remarkably little support from Church authorities these days. It is small wonder that many of them are thinking seriously of abandoning moderation. They have come to believe regretfully and reluctantly that their position may not be tenable much longer. They have always seen their task as one of mediation so that the forces of healthy progress can indeed assert themselves.

The moderates constitute a group that has respect for the accomplishments and authentic traditions of the Church. It is unquestioned in its loyalty and in its desire to serve the Church fully and well. To alienate this group is to destroy the link that prevents a more acrid and complete polarization within the Church itself. Church leaders must avail themselves of the help of those who have both the intelligence and the will to assist them in the tasks of renewal. The dissolution of the center, however, is one of the clear phenomena of the present moment. Many moderates have come to believe that when the chips are down authoritarian minds in the Church react much as Moscow did in relationship to the burgeoning spirit of freedom in Czechoslovakia. This is to destroy their hope. To destroy that is to eliminate one real source of hope for the whole Church.

It is probably true that mass apostasy is more a journalistic dream than a genuine possibility for the Catholic

Church at this time in history. The institution, despite the publicity, is probably secure because of the powerful social and personal identification that is inherent in being a Catholic. To preserve this is not the same as freeing a people to live more fully the life of the Spirit. It will be a sad day indeed when encouragement is so scarce that the great possibilities for God's people reaching "the full measure of manhood in Christ Jesus" are deflected or postponed out of fear. The institution may be preserved, but at the tremendous risk that it will be an echoing and empty fortress, where the Spirit could find neither room nor comfort.

Form Follows Function

In that remarkable document, "The Church in the Modern World," the assembled bishops of the Catholic Church displayed a rare sensitivity to the subtle processes of history. They suggested that "the human race is involved in a new stage in history," and went on to note that "we can already speak of a true cultural and social transformation." As members of a General Church Council, itself called, perhaps unconsciously, as a response to the dynamics of change, they became conscious of a quality of newness in man's mid-century experience. They had caught hold of the dominant truth of our time: man's institutions are challenged either to renew themselves or to suffer slow but sure disintegration.

This era demands a readiness to face the facts, especially about institutional forms, and to remodel them so that they may bear the weight of the human experience which they are called to channel and express. In the face of this challenge to structure, many people within the Church have developed what the German author Thomas Mann has characterized as a "sympathy for the abyss." There is no shortage of the prophets of doomsday. Their apocalytic vision seems to encourage others to hurl themselves into the abyss, or to give themselves over to gazing into it with agonizing self-pity. This is the mistake of those who sense the challenge to the renovation of ecclesiastical structures but misinterpret it as the end of Christianity, if not of the world.

Archimedes, the Greek mathematician, once said, "Give me a place to stand and I will move the world." If we are to bridge the abyss which seems to yawn before us, then we must have a place to stand in order that we can see things in perspective. There is another side to the abyss and man's energies must be given over to reaching it. The eschatological orientation of the Church is not meant to be a mournful interest in the last things as much as a lively commitment to the next things. Churchmen and churchwomen everywhere need a place to stand so that they can understand what has happened to bring about such drastic upheaval in the Church. The Church, after all, was supposed to be a rock, firm and resistant to the eroding tides of history. If one takes a closer look at a rock, however, one discovers that its inner reality is a mass of swirling atoms. So it is with the Church, which is hardly a steadfast but dead pile of stones. It is rather a dynamic communion of human persons.

Most people in the Church have not had a place to stand from which to view the Church as an institution, caught up with all other human institutions, in a massive challenge to modify and improve its structures. What has occurred in the Church has seemed more like a random or accidental event. Living with eyes focused only on the Church, many have failed to see it against the background of the universe in which it is set. As a result many within the Church feel that the tremors have somehow been caused through their own fault. They feel guilty and indict themselves as somehow responsible for the disturbing changes in the Church whose change-lessness they had prized.

The Church lives on the same geological fault of history with the rest of mankind. The wonder would be if the institutional forms of the Catholic Church went unques-tioned during a period when those of the rest of the world were being sharply challenged. The clearest truth of our age is that man has reached a point in history in which all institutional forms, no matter how well they have served man in the past, must be reshaped if they are to be suitable vehicles for human experience in the future. From Moscow, troubled with discipline in its ring of satellites, to Washington, where men speculate about the need to rewrite parts of the Constitution, there is ample evidence for this truth. The great centers of learning, formerly immune from questioning, are now barricaded symbols of the internal convulsions of institu-tions in our age. In the United States, political con-ventions, which have always been a revered part of Amer-icana, have clearly exhausted their vitality as democratic forms.

Even as these lines are written, the entrepreneurs of the sacred national pastime, baseball, have fired their commissioner as a first step in "totally restructuring the game." The testimony to changing institutions ranges from the constitutional conventions being called by many states to the disappearance of the family doctor, whose friendly rounds have been absorbed by group and clinic practice. All of these underscore the fact that we live in an age of institutional reformulation.

Those who fear for the relevance of the Church would have more to fear if the Church had somehow escaped this challenge. It would mean that the Church had so isolated itself from the course of history that it could no longer reverberate to the rhythms of the world in which it found itself. It is a healthy thing for the Church to find itself in anguish over its structure. This signifies that it is alive and well and living in the world of reality. If it had remained unstirred by the currents of the time, then its somnolence and rigidity would have proclaimed its final and complete irrelevance. As it is, it fittingly shares the agonies of the age. While this is painful, it is reassuring and hopeful at the same time.

Why has this era of challenge to institutions come about? The world has reached, according to some theorists, what can be characterized as a turbulent environment. The characteristics of a turbulent environment are these:

1. There is the widespread development of interdependent organizations which, because of their size and interrelationship, cause problems of themselves which did not exist before they came into being. Neither man's air nor his water are as fresh as they once were. These forms of pollution are by-products of this kind of industrial development. Men are beginning to realize the importance of the delicate balance in the environment which, quite unthinkingly, men can disturb profoundly. All man has to do is kill one strain of fish in order to set off a chain of events which makes it impossible to fish in a lake at all for years. If he fails to maintain the ecological balance in his forests and his fields, he may put to death his sources of life.

It is a strange phenomenon because nobody

planned it that way. Large cities rise and suddenly begin to rot from the inside out. For the first time in history man's cities are not perceived as places of safety but as scenes of danger. The problem is complicated because the largeness of the corporate structures which give rise to these problems makes it almost impossible to hold any individual or group of individuals responsible for their side-effects.

2. There is great interdependence between these organizations and the economic facets of society. What happens in one organization eventually has its effect on all other organizations and on society as well. This has repercussions for the whole economic well-being of the nation. A wage strike in one industry sets off the all too familiar wage-price spiral across many other industries. This self-heating phenomenon eventually touches everyone through the inflationary effect on the currency of the country. There is consequent governmental regulation and legal intervention in an effort to maintain some kind of balance in this elaborately interlocking system.

3. There is great emphasis on research and development. The balance sheets of most large companies show that more than a fair share of profits are plowed back into research and development every year. This aims at developing new products and new techniques and necessitates the built-in obsolescence in so many of man's products. Technical know-how is translated into commerce at a staggering rate. When man can make something or do something dif-

ferently, he hardly ever resists the temptation no matter what the consequences are. Thus, the Radio Corporation of America recently announced that of the twelve thousand products it now markets, half were unknown just ten years ago. The most important consequences of research and development are that they accelerate the pace of change and development described in the first two characteristics of a turbulent society.

4. There is the development of an electronic environment, the dreams of McLuhan come true. This makes it possible for man to communicate rapidly and efficiently. For the first time in history, men in very different parts of the world can participate, in some way at least, in the very same event. Millions of Americans and Europeans attended the funeral of Robert F. Kennedy through the selective eye of the television camera and with the help of orbiting satellites. For years Americans have seen at suppertime the blood and gore that took place in Vietnam that very morning.

The development of sophisticated mass communication constantly diminishes the time lapse between the discovery of new information or the occurrence of an important event and its transmission on a global scale to a great part of the human race. The difficulty is that the time is also diminished in which man can absorb and understand the significance of either the information or the event. There is no intervening generation to reflect upon and to interpret history which now comes fresh to everybody in the same instant.

The analysts of the turbulent environment suggest that when these conditions are reached human institutions are challenged and under threat. A reordered world demands a reordering of the structures of society. The familiar designs, which may have served admirably for years, must now be renewed if they are to serve man effectively in the future. In effect, man is asked not if but when he will renew his institutions. The accumulated force of these cultural changes demands a rethinking and a reformulation of the political, economic, educational, and even recreational structures of society. Because man has reached this point of development there is a widespread need to redesign the structures which are meant to house his humanity.

Man has a challenge but he also has a choice. He can either busy himself with the task of institutional renewal or, failing to understand the times, he can reject the opportunity. The consequences of rejecting this challenge are not very helpful. If he chooses to remain passive, this will not exempt his institutional forms from the effects of the turbulent environment. They will break down, perhaps gradually at first, because they no longer respond to the needs of the times.

In many ways the collapse of familiar structures in our time resembles the thunderclap disintegration of an old barn. These barns dot any rural landscape. Worn and used, they have retained the outlines of a farm building even though nature has weathered its substance away. The process of decay is a long and slow one. The internal collapse, however, comes in an instant. It may even surprise the neighbors who thought that the building would stand forever. This is very much the way it has been for some structures within the Church. They have maintained the outlines of their form even though they have slowly but surely been disintegrating toward the final point of collapse over the last several years. It is no longer a question of repairing a building or shoring up worn but still serviceable walls. The time for that has long since passed. The only thing that can be done is to clear away the debris and to build a new structure.

Man, however, with his buildings falling around him can respond by nimbly dodging the snowy showers of plaster and roofing. He can, in other words, choose to be passive and defensive rather than open and responsive. This is indeed the point which Herbert Marcuse has made about the conditions of Western industrialized society. He notes that they approximate roughly the conditions described by the students of the turbulent environment. Men can be defensive in this situation in several ways. They can, for example, dissociate themselves from the events and their culture. No phrase is now more common than "I couldn't care less." Today's hero "never loses his cool" as he avoids the investment of himself in the problems of his culture. This is by no means an unusual response in view of the frustrations of the day. It is sometimes seen in the Church in the simple-minded insularity of those who content themselves with the conviction that the Church is not of this world and should pay no heed to it, other than to stand in judgment over it. It is the response of those who cling to the vestige of the privileges granted to priests and religious at a time when the institutional structure still supported the Catholic experience. It is the response of those who think we can find some supposedly more perfect and separate style of life which ignores and isolates itself from the realistic struggles of mankind. Many Catholics are among the most ardent supporters of a resurgent nationalism in the name of patriotism, which chauvinistically puts to death any missionary sense of sharing their faith with others.

A second form of defensiveness finds society breaking itself into pieces through fractionation. This is a phenomenon by which certain segments of society can move forward and successfully leave others behind. Thus white, affluent, middle-class America can move ahead and leave behind the black and the other minority groups that are still so shackled by poverty that they limp in their search for the decent life. So powerful is the affluent segment of society that it can successfully move on in this non-integrated fashion. This is paralleled in the Church, which identifies itself too exclusively with the ascendant aspects of society, with the "making it" generation of postwar Catholics who have come a long way since their grandparents dropped their bags at Ellis Island. It is fractionation in classic form when churchmen can say that questions of race relations and economic justice for less affluent groups in society are not moral but political and legal matters. Someone once told me that there is nothing better in life than being a rich South American Catholic who with relatively undisturbed conscience enjoys blessings of both worlds in staggering abundance. It is, however, not too bad to be a slightly mortgaged suburban North American Catholic whose Church does not upset him with any severe questions about his obligation to the society or the world in which he lives.

The third form of defense against the challenges of institutional redesign is seen in a trivialization of the environment. This, according to Marcuse, is manifested in superficiality. We live in a society where a man can order a car and have it painted with one of more than a hundred different shades of color. He can choose from almost as many options in accessory equipment. He can have colored television and a bewildering choice in clothes, vacations, and entertainment. This kind of society responds in abundance to the least important needs of man. At the same time it cannot solve the problem of poverty. Neither can it guarantee that every citizen will have a proper education, a healthy diet, or adequate housing. It is this situation which Marcuse describes as "one-dimensional society," inhabited by "one-dimensional man." One-dimensional society can give man a wide variety of what is not essential and suffocates the needs in him which most demand liberation.

If Western industrialized society reflects the descriptions of Marcuse accurately, it is not hard to find similar reflections of superficiality within the Church itself. At a time of great stress, there are many churchmen who are comfortable in dealing with the least important aspects of life while they let the more important ones go. Much renewal in the Church has been characterized by preoccupation with the superficial. It has not dealt radically or substantially with the fundamental issues about the nature and needs of man to which it should give its full energies and attention. One need only thumb through some current religious periodicals or diocesan newspapers to find how given over we still are to the minor rubrics and observances which are distantly related, if at all, to the nature of the Christian life itself. It is a wonderful thing to have so many minor points to occupy so many people. It is something like the wonderfully busy personnel in remote South American airports who, if the planes did not run late, would have very little to do. As it is, they keep enthusiastically busy stamping various pieces of paper, making announcements, and looking intensely at the empty skies. In the Church, the authoritarian bureaucrat has been marvelously prepared to respond to the least important needs of men. He serves the organization well but is incapable of reacting positively to the deepest religious needs of people.

It is strangely true that much pain is connected with minor points of life. Evidence abounds that the institutionalized aspects of the Church attenuated the horizons of its people, especially of priests and religious, so that they made a heavy investment of their lives in things of relatively minor importance. At the same time they failed to develop sufficient understanding of life's major values. One clear sign of this is the degree of emotion associated with small events. One cannot explain the amount of feeling connected with determining the time people get up and go to bed or the kind of clothes they wear in carrying out their jobs unless somewhere along the line a very false set of values has been emphasized. This is basically a defensive maneuver. It is a clear indication, perceived a long time ago by many shrewd observers, that something in the familiar institutional structures of the Church badly needs examination.

Indeed, a whole kingdom was created, something like the fantasies of Tolkien, in which Catholics lived for years. It was minutely structured and was inhabited by a race of people whose existence came mainly from the lively imaginations of canon lawyers into whose charge the codification of the moral life somehow fell.

Positive law is a great achievement of reflective man. In the Church, however, regulations, and their observance, became a substitute for the free life of mature people in the Spirit. A great many ordinances are needed when people are presumed to be incapable of forming their own consciences about their manner of life. It is not to deny the need for religious and moral principles to note

the excessive burden of decrees that came to wear the
wayfaring Christian to the ground.

Those obsessed with legalism did a splendid job, according to their needs, in extending deadening bylaws
to the human experience of Christians. It is, incidentally,
to the credit of the Canon Law Society of America that
it has given leadership in pointing out the need for
drastic reformation in the laws of the Church.

In any case, the carefully structured juridic world of
Catholicism is no more. Good people do not take it too
seriously any more. In its golden age it was full of
fictional characters such as *fugitivi* and *peregrini*. The
great villain was the *excommunicatus vitandus*, the ex-
communicated person so pulsing with evil that he was to
be avoided by other Christians. It was filled with marvelously insignificant moral dilemmas, such as whether a
person living in a diocese bound by fasting regulations
could hold himself free from them if he would travel
later in the day to a diocese where they were not in
effect. Incredibly detailed suspensions could be leveled
on priests such as the classic set of regulations in a north-
eastern diocese. There a priest was suspended from his
functions if (a) he rode in a boat with a woman, (b) rode
in a boat from which a woman was water-skiing, or (c)
water-skied from a boat in which a woman was riding.
These seem properly ridiculous to anyone with a real
understanding of life but they are characteristic of the
chalk lines drawn around the lives of the servants of the
Church. The regulations that filled the lives of women
in the Church were even more detailed and more ridiculous. To require nuns to kneel in the chapel aisle during
their menstrual period, or to forbid them the use of sani-
tary napkins, are extreme but true examples of the
cramped kind of minds that could see evil in the most

natural of human experiences. It is perhaps small wonder
that priests and religious developed a strange and distorted outlook on the lives of those they were meant to
serve with understanding and compassion.

There were awesome phenomena in this closed world,
such as *morose delectation,* a vaguely described attitude
that was always dangerous, even if nobody ever quite
understood it. The leading citizens of this world were a
certain Caius and Bertha, the names frequently employed in the moral casuistry of the time. This couple
managed to get themselves into an enormous amount of
trouble. The alert student, however, had an armful of
legalisms by which he could pass judgment on their
spiritual condition. The twofold effect, an undeniably
valid principle, was always at hand. The difficulty lay
in the fact that it was frequently discussed in examples
that were unrealistic. Could a winsome young virgin,
threatened by rape or mutilation by enemy hordes, throw
herself out a window to preserve her virtue? Could a
pilot crash his plane into an enemy ship if his intention
was not to kill himself? It was an unreal world, full of
bloodless and emotionless persons, and it generated an
unreal attitude toward the real problems of human beings. Full of precision and punishments, this mind set
could deal only with abstract persons. It dealt with man
in the legal but not the human condition. The structure
of this world had a fine mesh covering which left little
room for the action of the Spirit.

One could find, for example, in that most impenetrable
of moral theology tracts, justice and rights, a legalistic
horn of plenty. The "treasure-trove" principle, for example, went into great detail about the ownership of
accidentally discovered goods. Under what conditions
could the finder keep them? Suppose you rented the

land? What about the original owner, or the man with legal title to the property on which they were found? Such challenges to common sense made the mind reel after a while. Those tempted to cynicism summarized the hundreds of pages of the tract by saying, "If it's not yours, give it back." The worst result of such confounding detail was the effect it had on developing the clerical outlook, from which man could only be seen through a latticework of laws. The conditioned cleric who translated religious belief and practice for the People of God, could understand what was legally just without having any feeling for justice in the affairs of mankind. In studying the nature of faith as applied to life, he knew the difference between heresy and apostasy but had little grasp of what it meant to believe either in God or in his fellow man. So in the tract on charity, he could wrestle with the problem of whether one was bound in justice to love others, and fail to penetrate the mysteries of human sharing and responsible love. The growing irrelevance of the opinions of clergymen about real-life issues arose precisely because the priest was trained and lived in an irrelevant and largely imaginary world.

It is this world of solutions for which there were no human problems that has been repudiated in our day. This is an example of an entire structure of institutionalized Christianity which is being challenged by men whose needs are no longer met by it. The slowness to recognize this, the suspicious regard in which younger moral theologians are held, the onerous and secret revision of canon law despite the splendid guidelines provided by American sources—all of these are the signs of institutionally oriented churchmen who cannot understand that their attitudes are being questioned, not because of irreligion on the part of men, but because of a basic irrelevance of their own.

This structured world gave Catholic people in general a false sense of security about what religious belief demanded of them. It was fish on Fridays, Mass on Sundays, and a host of other things that could be ticked off to the delight of the legalist's mind. One wishes he could speak of the legalist's heart instead. These structures of Church life supplied people with a massively detailed program almost guaranteed to develop obsessive-compulsive neuroses, while it failed to shed enough light on the urgent questions of the way men should live with and love one another. It is no surprise that once these accidentals were revised, there was a great sense of loss and a consequent amount of confusion in the minds of many Catholics. What religion mostly meant to them, the strict observance of regulations, was suddenly swept away. They were left less than well prepared to deal with the question of the formation of their own conscience in the face of life's dilemmas. It is small wonder that there has been so much agonizing over the question of freedom of conscience. The previous structures of Catholic life never permitted men to confront the real issues of life at sufficient depth to make the formation of their own conscience a viable task for them. The Church formed their conscience and supplied the rules. That seemed to be the function of the Church, which created myriad forms in order to carry this out. These are the forms that have failed as men have had to face new and deeper questions about life and its direction in the post-conciliar era.

That is also why the present era has been so bewildering and frustrating for so many churchmen, especially those leaders who have been trained extensively in canon law. Their training prepared them to carry out the functions that seemed to vitalize the forms of the Church of yesterday. They were very good at documents, dispensations, and the requirements about reading the banns of marriage. Because these forms are now clearly inadequate to express the very basic questions about liberty, justice, and love which are so much at the center of life, these leaders are left with tools that are no longer effective. This explains, however, why they continue to use the approaches of the past, in the form of condemnations, warnings, and the detailed prescriptions of the expectations of personal behavior, with which they were so familiar and so comfortable in the past. It is why it is so difficult for them to speak clearly about freedom of conscience. This also explains why so many quite sincere Catholics no longer pay a great deal of attention to what they have to say when they speak in this language. At the same time it makes understandable why so many in authority are threatened by the challenges of institutional renewal. They are confused because what they were good at, administration, responds to a need that people do not now experience. They are consequently no longer rewarded by their activity.

The Church had somehow reversed the famous dictum of the architect Frank Lloyd Wright that "form follows function." Instead of trying to ascertain what the function of the Church should be in responding to the needs of man, churchmen provided Christians with a detailed form of life and told them that they must function as best they could out of this framework. This was bound to break down sooner or later. There were few, however, who could perceive this. It is obvious that the task of this generation is to understand the function of the Church as fully as possible and then to oversee the development of forms which best allow this function to be

carried out. If one has even an approximate understanding of the function of the Church, one can allow a great
variety of forms if these promote the mission of the
Church to mankind.

To understand this as the proper challenge of the
day is a far different thing from envisioning a Christianity that will be free-flowing and protoplasmic in nature. Man, by his very nature, needs structures. These
must match his nature so that they can truly express his
spirit. The contemporary task is not just to pull down the
rotting structures of the past. It is far more urgent to lay
the foundations and start raising the walls of the structures that will accommodate the Church effectively in
the coming century. The Church shares this problem with
all the other great institutions of mankind. If it fails
to understand this, it can only stubbornly hold on to
forms which are no longer useful because they obstruct
rather than facilitate the function of the Church. It is
not a bad thing, nor is it a random or accidental event,
that we have entered the era of institutional renewal.
The Vatican Council itself was a response, perhaps not
fully conscious, to the cultural forces which have presented this challenge to all men. It is not the fault of
any individual or group that the older formulations no
longer serve the Church or mankind effectively. The
only mistake would be to misunderstand the nature of
the problem, and thereby fail to get a place to stand from
which one can see these processes in adequate perspective.

John Gardner, the head of the Urban Coalition, wrote
recently from the viewpoint of the twenty-third century:

Men came to demand more and more of their
institutions—and with greater intransigence. But

while aspirations leapt ahead, human institutions remained sluggish . . . because of failure
to design institutions capable of continuous renewal, twentieth century society showed as-
tonishing sclerotic streaks. Twentieth century
institutions were caught in the savage crossfire
between uncritical lovers and unloving critics.
On the one hand, those who loved their institutions tended to smother them in the embrace
of death, loving their rigidities more than their
promise, shielding them from life-giving criticism. On the other side, there arose a breed of
critics without love, skilled in demolition but
untutored in the arts by which human institutions are nurtured and strengthened and made
to flourish.

New York *Times*, July 27, 1968

The point of choice is before the Church. It need not
bewail the inadequacies of past formulations to recognize
that they have outlived their usefulness. Neither can the
Church afford a rebellious, New Left-like revolt that
would level all the structures of the Church and call
this an accomplishment. Neither the uncritical lovers nor
the unloving critics are willing to deal with the question
of the function of the Church as it prepares itself for
the next century.

The Church proclaims salvation and offers itself as the
servant of all men. The Church is for man. If it is to
serve him it must understand him deeply and respond
to all his needs adequately. This is the function of the
Church and the forms of its response flow from a comprehension of this. They can be quite varied. That indeed would match man much more truly than the rigid

and spent forms which saw man so narrowly and allowed such little room for persons to reach their individual fullness in Christ.

The great block to institutional renewal in the Church are those men and women who have not shed the closed and clerical cast of mind which cannot tell the difference between what is essential and what is accidental to the life of the Spirit. This kind of person also mistakes the disintegrating institutional structures of the Church for the disintegration of Christianity itself. They can only commit themselves to the preservation of structures which impede rather than further the function of the Church. But form follows function and this generation must deepen its understanding of the Church as mission to mankind. It must then oversee the positive development of structures that will enable the Church once more to share its good news joyfully with the world.

The Guilt Machine Breaks Down

One of the functions which the Church carried out quite effectively over the years was that of making people feel guilty. This was not the same as helping people to develop a sense of sin. Neither did it give them the courage to look deeply within themselves and to face their true personal orientation toward life. It is far easier to make people slaves of neurotic guilt than to free them to take on the perilous responsibilities of life. Nothing is so facilely manipulated as a sense of guilt in believers who have been conditioned to look on their religious leaders as the possessors of the keys to individual and social conscience.

The person who can control the feelings of guilt in another has a strange and all-pervading power over him. By balancing a vision of the fiery terrors of the hereafter against the promises of paradise, a preacher can exact from people a fearful obedience to whatever code of morality he wishes to propose. That churchmen have succumbed to this temptation may be understandable, given the weaknesses of human nature. This does not make it justifiable, however, and no amount of explanation can make up for the abuses of religious authority that have played upon the guilt feelings of human beings. This includes holy rollers and holy fathers. That this has been a style of relationship between priests and people is undeniable. It is only now, with the bonds of neurotic guilt loosening, that we can see how destructive it has been to the process of full religious maturity. The guilt machine is breaking down and with it the sure control over behavior that some churchmen exercised so deftly in the past.

A partial explanation of this is found in the old-style training of clergymen, who learned endless categories of sins even if they did not develop a sensitivity to the real meaning of sinfulness. The imposition of the logic of law on the questions of how a person lived his life in relationship to others established the schemata of textbook order but obscured an understanding of the struggle of human persons for fullness of life. Symptomatic of this was the fact that in many seminaries the moral theology courses came to be taught by men whose training was fundamentally in canon law. They were very good at handling the distinctions between formal and material sin, material sin really being no sin at all. They could go on at great length about merely penal laws. By some involuted rationalization the individual did not have to obey penal laws unless he was caught breaking them. It is small wonder that the average priest became absorbed in the data about sin and its subdivisions and was so unequipped to deal with sinful men. That is why Jean Paulhan, the supposed author of the erotic *The Story of O,* said, "I think it should be read by all priests because they do not have a sufficient sense of sin."

The cleric, programmed in the categories of moral and

venial sins, was also prepared to be a judge about the behavior of men. To man's behavior he could only apply the measurement he had been given in his courses of theology. The emphasis was very much on individual acts detached from the human persons who performed them. The failure to develop a sense of sin arose largely from the priest's lack of feeling for the human person. Psychology and psychiatry were suspect and often described by threatened legalists as the disciplines that were trying to eliminate sin. On the contrary, the insights of these professions, insofar as they deepen an understanding of man, also deepen an understanding of a person's motivation and responsibility for his actions.

This also explains why many clergymen became more absorbed in what man could do wrong than in the encouragement of what he could do right. It was not only difficult for him to develop a sense of sin, it was also hard for the priest to have any feeling for the efforts of people to grow in doing good. At the same time the clergyman was placed on a pedestal, some of the foundation of which he erected himself, a position from which the temptations to authoritarian behavior were very many. He was the man with the answers about good and evil, more a ruler than a leader of the Christian community. This naturally reinforced the dependence of his people on him and slowed the proper development of their own sense of judgment about their lives.

It was from this authoritarian plateau that people heard over and over again a distorted theology of guilt. What was good or bad was so because of a judgment of authority. There was no need, with such judgments available, for people to wrestle with their own consciences about the consequences of their behavior. This tended to keep people at the level of personal development where their religious values came mostly from the outside. What they believed in and how they lived depended on what somebody else told them. Many Catholics remained moral children because they went through life with extrinsic values. They had neither the opportunity nor the encouragement to internalize these values for themselves. The good life came from following the rules resolutely. That is why the hallmark of the Catholic became attendance at Mass on Sunday and abstinence from meat on Friday. These were powerful emblems, enhancing because of the disciplinary demands inherent in them, of being a good Catholic. These and a whole roster of other behaviors, if faithfully observed, kept one in good standing and assured the individual of a safe passage to heaven. All too often the weightier things of life, such as the development of a Christian sense of social justice and service to the world, were ignored.

It was the heyday of the fiery preacher and the wrathful retreat master. Someone should put together a book of the wild tales that scared people half to death even though they did not promote much in the way of mature religious behavior. Missions and retreats pivoted on the fears of hell. The most farfetched and unforgettable analogies were devised and spoken in a properly quaking voice to describe the eternity of punishment which awaited the sinner. It did not matter that he had led a good life up until the last day of it. That final and fatal misstep carried him over the brink where he could roast in remorse but could never undo his last offense.

I can still hear the quiet in the whole Church as a preacher in my childhood conjured up a picture of Gibraltar, touched only every other decade by the wing of a passing bird. By the time Gibraltar was worn away by these aggressive sea gulls, eternity would still be in its first moment. These preachers, who developed a splendid vindictive style, also exulted in describing the flames that burned but did not destroy the sinner. There wasn't even much comfort in the writings of St. Theresa of the Child Jesus, the gentle Little Flower, whose vision of souls falling into hell like the leaves from the autumnal trees was a familiar and terrifying quote.

As I think back on the Church full of husbands and wives struggling to make ends meet during the depression years, most of them kindly people trying to do the best they could with life, I am sure that someone will have to answer someday for the cheap melodramatics which they got as a substitute for religious instruction. One can breathe a sigh of relief that the guilt machine which cast such a spell over a relatively innocent audience has now broken down.

There was hardly anything in the Christian life which did not have dire consequences attached to it. Preachers could get lyrical about doing what they called "servile work on Sundays." Frozen in my position as an altar boy in the sanctuary I listened in awe to the announcement that any lady who so much as dared to rinse out her stockings on Sunday would turn away from her washtub with "hands dripping with mortal sin." The big build-up during the nights of the parish mission was toward that evening on which would be discussed the source of all sin, sex itself. On that evening the preacher had a new air of solemnity. Even we altar boys were enjoined to stay in the sacristy while this adult confrontation proceeded. In the ways of small boys, however, we managed to hear a good deal through the crack in the door. It is a wonder that people returned to church at all, so condemned were they for having sexual feelings or for wishing to express their love for each other in a healthy way. The genesis of many unhealthy Catholic attitudes toward sex surely depended on the views communicated in this kind of conference.

I have heard the conference repeated in many different ways since that time. It was a favorite of high school retreats, strategically placed to ensure that students would come to all the conferences so as not to miss the spine tingling of the discussion of sex. Here again, horror stories abounded. In fact, these seemed to substitute pretty much for telling people anything factual about the matter that was supposed to be discussed. Kissing a girl, or even getting into the same general ambiance with her, was almost always "an occasion of sin." How the rhetoric would soar as the preacher described a boy and a girl necking in what was then called the rumble seat of a car, not knowing that the bridge was out on the road ahead. "They slipped from the leather seats of the car to the fiery chairs of hell!" the speaker would thunder in a tone that emphasized his reluctance at even being called on to speak of sex. Better still, for oratorical purposes, was the young man who had been too intimate with his girl friend and who later that night was struck by lightning, its fire having burned the sign of the cross into his chest.

Later on, I would hear college students told off by an irate preacher who said that "dealing with you makes me feel like I am swimming in a sea of semen." The list of these outrageous examples could go on and on. They merely illustrate the general attitude of the clergyman as prosecuting attorney bent on getting his indictment from an audience properly fearful of eternal punishment. I am afraid that many people were conditioned in the Christian life by these showers of fire and brimstone. It is no surprise that they developed neurotic feelings of guilt. They could so easily step aside from the path of virtue and lose everything, even at the last moment, before the judgment seat of God. The ideal seemed to keep people from doing things and to make them concentrate on carrying out the obligations, quite limitless in number, of being good Catholics. There was little sense of liberation for people who were dominated by fear. The world was a wild and wicked place and the Catholic could pass through it only with his eyes firmly fixed on his heavenly goal. These methods were themselves wicked and caused suffering that still lingers in the lives of many people. People were hardly helped to love themselves when they were enjoined so strenuously to chain the evil beasts within them. That this was unhealthy is now unquestionable but that it was used extensively is undeniable. The consequences for people who were given a distorted understanding of themselves and their own humanity are difficult to measure fully. The stains of sin were resistant to being washed out, no matter how well-intentioned the sinner was. He could painfully and slowly acquire indulgences and quarantines, those mysterious and somewhat inexplicable entities attached to a multitude of practices and prayers.

Indeed, the preacher who could so subtly tap the feelings of guilt in people waxed strong on what was prohibited. By a strange set of values, he was the same preacher who could give heavy emphasis to at least one positive thing, donating money to the Church. "Your good Catholic," a hoary old pastor once told me, in a summation of his life's wisdom, "is your contributing Catholic." Sin on the one hand and the solicitation of funds on the other became the staple diet for many Catholics. These items tended to crowd off the agenda a fuller response to the needs of the people themselves.

Perhaps it was this distortion of Christian life that made it somewhat unappealing to many sensitive Catholics such as the many writers and intellectuals who moved out of the Church during the years when such values were emphasized.

Religion did not center on the way a person related to himself and to other people as much as it did on carrying out all the specifications of the law. They were the way to security, whether it was through the route of the First Fridays, faithfully and consecutively attended (break the string of nine and one had to begin all over again), or the novenas and rosaries, some of which were keyed more to anxiety about, rather than a peaceful faith in, God.

All this was extremely controlling and certainly satisfying for churchmen who wanted a palpable measure of faith in the behavior of their people. It tended to keep the people passive and receptive. It did little to help them think for themselves. It was controlling because of the massive use of fear which was balanced by the guaranteed visas to a better world that would be accorded to those who are faithful to their obligations. It was in this atmosphere that preoccupation about sex became such a corrosive element in Catholic life. It was also in this atmosphere that so much obsessive-compulsive behavior developed in the name of religion.

If people were anxious, they could quiet their fears by carrying out carefully all that was expected of them. To keep rules, to accept the pronouncements of the priest as practically infallible, would lessen the anxiety. Meanwhile the emphasis on repetitive acts developed a compulsive pattern of behavior. The worry about little things left little time for people to deepen their grasp of the fundamental Christian vision of life. It allowed little time to internalize their religion, to develop their consciences, and to see their relationship to their neighbor as the only sure evidence of the kind of love they had for God.

Indeed, human relationships were barely tolerable. They were full of dangers. The best things in life, the only things in life worthwhile, always ran the risk of being those dreadful occasions of sin. It was the delight, unconscious surely, of small minds to reinforce this obsessive symptomatic behavior. It was no surprise that many Catholics developed scrupulous consciences, always falling short and never able to measure up to the demands which their religion seemed to make on them. They could never do anything completely, never with the complete perfection that this stern and guilt-engendering religion demanded of them. Isolation is a typical reaction for the obsessive-compulsive personality. For Catholics, this expressed itself in an isolation from the world because they were unable to tolerate and deal positively with the ordinary feelings of life.

These techniques reached a zenith in some areas of the religious life where the master plan for perfection awaited those who subjected themselves to its training procedures. Somebody in the Church is responsible for doing terrible things to men and women in the name of making them perfect. Reinforced in a thousand ways by the dynamics of fear and guilt, men and women contorted themselves to the destruction of their own true personalities because they thought they were doing what was right. This whole monstrous machine, with all its convoluted inner workings, has exploded in the more mature and realistic religious expectation of Vatican II. The wreckage of the machinery is everywhere and some people misidentify it as the wreckage of the Church itself. Indeed, it had to be destroyed for the Church to find itself again.

It is against this whole structure of authoritarian conditioning that many Catholics have rebelled at the present time. Better-educated and more confident of their position in society, these Catholics feel liberated from the fears that once dominated them. They look now for the Church to respond to the full range of their needs in helping them to live the resurrected life. More conscious of social ills, they expect leadership from churchmen who can mobilize their energies for constructive participation in the transformation of society. This does not apply only to the younger generation, although they may be more deeply conscious of their commitment of service to mankind. Older people, too, look for the Church to help them live as Christians who are not merely the bearers of obligations or contributors to collection baskets. Many older people have come to trust their own Christian instincts more fully. As one lady in her sixties said recently, "For years I believed that eating meat on Friday was just as bad as murdering someone. I should never have believed it. And the bishops better not expect us to accept that sort of thing any more. There is more to life than that. I always thought there must be but I am sure of it now."

It is sadly true that in many areas Catholics who faithfully followed an earlier style of religious response, now find themselves without the broader vision or inspiration of the Christian life. These are the Catholics, up-to-date on their special obligations, who have never found religion affecting their attitudes toward life in general. These Catholics are reacting in the only way that they understand because they were not helped to form deeper religious convictions. They go to Mass and the sacraments but they actively oppose full rights for black men, are suspicious of the war on poverty and the need for welfare, and give strong support to extreme right-wing groups. It is difficult to blame them because the Church formed them in isolation from a desperately poor and weary world.

The seemingly positive results of the emphasis of an earlier era were badly misjudged by shortsighted leaders who must never have expected their people to grow up. A generation ago it was proudly said that "the Catholic Church is a hard one to live in but a good one to die in." This may be no less true today but for different reasons. It was indeed difficult to live in a structure which demanded so many faithful responses of external religious behavior. There was a satisfaction because of the reduction of anxiety that came with carrying out these prescriptions exactly. It is still difficult to be a Catholic but now it is because one must live with a broader vision of Christian responsibility in the face of anxieties that are no longer worked off so readily. To be a Catholic today one must struggle with issues of belief and commitment which transcend the observance of a multitude of regulations.

Many Church leaders seem unprepared for the day when the effects of developing a system of Catholic education would be fully experienced. Catholic schools, once the laboratories in which the first conditioning toward avoiding a guilt-filled life took place, have also been liberated from a self-contained set of values. They have opened themselves to a less defensive stance toward the secular educational world and have worked for a mature grasp of the ideals by which adult Catholics must live.

It is the old-time religion of "hitting the confessional box" and "hitting the communion rail" that sickens rather than attracts young people. In large measure they turn away from a guilt-producing form of religious life, with its trappings and practices, because Catholic educators have given them a broader perspective on life. Gone forever is the Catholic college atmosphere in which religion and the athletic conquest of Protestant schools were co-extensive. Gone with it is the sex-obsessed religious preparation which identified the elimination of masturbation with the virtuous life.

The reaction of conscientious Catholics against authoritarian pronouncements in our day is not a sign of rampant unbelief as much as it is an assertion of the desire to take on the responsibilities of adult Christians. A prime example is the formation of conscience, long defended in theory, but only gingerly allowed to Catholics in practice. The Church must meet man's needs for the kind of education in principle and psychological preparation in freedom that allow him to exercise this responsibility. Freedom of conscience, of its very essence, can only be employed by the individual. It is the situation in which he makes his actions his own, in which he is truly responsible for the probity of his actions and the quality of his relationships. To obfuscate this right, to hedge it with qualifications, is to make evident that churchmen are uneasy about allowing persons to be free. It means that they are cautious about allowing people to be fully responsible for their actions. This kind of fear leads to awkward reactions when individuals claim this right for themselves. It is an insult to people ready for adult responsibilities to tell them, as one Stephen Decatur-like cardinal did recently, to follow authority whether it is right or wrong.

Many leaders in the Church are obviously unprepared to relate themselves maturely to people who are unafraid of taking responsibility for judging the moral quality of their own behavior. They turn instead to oiling up the machinery that produced guilt abundantly and thereby effectively controlled the consciences of others. They must learn that the present ineffectiveness of this device, as outmoded as the instruments of the Inquisition, is a hopeful sign. Christians are ready for responsibility and they will not easily settle for an unsatisfying passivity in the sacred business of living their lives in the sight of God.

The demands of the age are on those people in the Church who are charged with leading it to the freedom of the sons of God, not to bringing its people back into submission. It is their problem to see that the moral educational practice of the Church is appropriately informed and mature. Their older responses are no longer effective and these churchmen must confront their own needs to resurrect them at this time. The guilt machine has indeed broken down, a fact for which all Christians should be thankful. It leaves before the Church the challenge of responding to one of man's most profound needs, the development of a free and mature conscience.

The Line of Defense

The defenses employed by human beings resemble the
Maginot line, that stretch of pill boxes which supposedly
made France secure in 1940. The defense of that cele-
brated line was an illusion because the fixed guns had
no flexibility. All the enemy had to do was sweep around
and behind them. So it is with the lines of psychological
defense which human persons erect to protect their idea
of themselves. These defenses are more illusion than reality, more impressive to those who possess them than to
those who observe them. People can see through them
and penetrate them even when the defender thinks he
is most secure. The tragedy of defense mechanisms is
that they often fool only the persons who employ them.
In the long run they are not a substantial basis for relationship to life.

No one is a stranger to exaggerating a good story or
to making himself a leading figure in an incident in
which he was really only an observer. Every man has
been known to tell a few self-enhancing white lies. Defenses become dangerous when individuals use them as
a major mode of adjustment to life. They then present

a false self, a mask of personality which does not serve well in the process of making good relationships with other people. The truth shows through, even when the defensive person will not face it himself. A heavy penalty is paid for this faulty presentation of the self because the relationships of the defensive individual are seldom deep. They cannot, therefore, be a source of growth either for himself or for others in his life.

We live in an age in which critics have made much of the need for truthfulness and basic honesty in the Church. These critics have seen through the Maginot line-like defenses that churchmen have all too often employed. They understand that a façade is a weak and inadequate face for the Church to present to the world. Indeed, one of the most profound dynamics of the Second Vatican Council arose from the willingness of many churchmen to put aside defenses and to look deeply into the truth about the Church. It is this willingness to be open and honest that we prize highly both in individuals and institutions. When honesty is present, imperfections are tolerable. When dishonesty becomes characteristic of adjustment, then the pretended perfection of the person or the institution becomes sickening and quite intolerable. The extensive use of defenses makes it impossible for the Church to establish saving relationships with mankind. It becomes too intent on protecting itself and on denying fault or failure. It therefore loses credibility in the eyes of everyone.

Defenses are used by human beings when they have a false picture of themselves which is suddenly threatened by a challenge that reveals the truth which the defenses disguise. It is like the situation in which a person who is truly lazy survives in life by comforting himself with the notion that he works very hard. Most observers can easily see through his constant complaints about his difficult schedule and his self-advertised long hours at his daily tasks. There are, however, moments of truth when this cherished self-described zeal is attacked by somebody who can tolerate the pretense no longer. This frequently happens when people have had a few drinks or in the course of an increasingly emotional argument. Suddenly the lazy man is challenged: "The real trouble with you is that you don't work hard at all! You just go around telling everybody you do!" This kind of statement gives rise to a picture of the individual which is inconsistent with the concept that he has held of himself. Its inconsistency makes it very threatening and causes him to experience anxiety. The vulnerably lazy person, somewhat like a self-sealing tire, characteristically reacts by marshaling his defenses. He must not allow into his consciousness a picture of himself which so contradicts what he wants to believe about himself.

The first thing such a challenged individual may do is to deny the accusation. "What do you mean, I don't work hard? Why, I am the hardest working person around here!" He may, employing another strategy, explain away the accusation. "The trouble with you is that you don't know the kind of work I have to do. You don't understand how much it demands of me." He may also turn the accusation around, in the knowledge that attack is always a good defense. "You're the one who is lazy," he might say, or "The trouble with you is that you're jealous of me." By adopting one of these postures, he has reassured himself about his self-image. He thereby eliminates anxiety by reducing the threat that arises from the inconsistency of the picture that someone else has presented to him. This is the typical function of the defense mechanisms. All of them share the quality of self-deception. This reveals itself either through denial or disguise.

Because the openness that was evident during the Second Vatican Council seems slowly being closed off, it is necessary to inspect the possible defenses which the Church uses to protect its image of itself. This surely goes against the way Christ preached and lived His life. It makes a mockery of the Church that is meant to be the home of truth. Consistent openness is clearly never easy. Honesty with oneself and with others is still the only valid basis for a Christian relationship to others. No man loves himself very much if he is afraid to take a good look at himself, or to admit and to attempt to correct his failings and to give himself to others in a transparently real way. The Church always succeeds when it is most open and unafraid of its human failings, because it is sure that it is the instrument of the Spirit.

It is the purpose of this chapter to reflect on some of the chief mechanisms of defense. They are used all too often by churchmen who are afraid of the truth and who put most of their energies into preserving notions about themselves or the Church which are not valid. They are very defensive in many of their actions, touchy about points of inquiry, and always explain away the challenges of a confrontation with the truth.

The most common type of defense is *rationalization*. Rationalization is the technique by which a person gives a good reason for what he does even if it is not the real reason. It is an explanation which may seem to be very good. He uses it because it reinforces the self-concept by which he lives. He likes to think well of himself and to believe that his motives are always of the highest order. Rationalization, however, does not signify "to act rationally" as much as it signifies the justification of actions which one has performed for reasons one does not like to admit.

Rationalizations have been used plentifully to explain away the difficulties and problems of the Church. Rationalization always puts the burden on someone else, on a menacing fate, or on contrary circumstances. The vocation shortage in the Church, for example, is rationalized with the common statement that people are no longer generous or that a secular spirit abounds. This sounds good, perhaps even plausible, but it merely hides rather than uncovers the true sources of explanation.

It is rationalization which leads people to say that those who raise questions about the decisions of the Church are weak in faith or are of a disobedient turn of mind. The same mechanism makes it possible to assert that those who leave the priesthood or the religious life are merely the malcontents or the misfits who should never have entered in the first place. If one can believe these things, one does not have to change because the fault lies outside oneself. If one maintains these defenses, one need not look deeper or even make an effort to uncover better explanations of the situations that are being dealt with. Rationalizations, of course, are not used merely by those in authority. They are frequently used by persons who are unwilling to inspect their own motivations. That is why it is easy to say "My superiors never understood me," or "The Church never did anything for me," when the truth may be somewhat different from these assertions.

The defense mechanisms overlap one another considerably. *Projection* is the second line of defense. An individual protects himself from recognizing his own bad qualities by projecting them out in some exaggerated form onto other people. One can then justify his own tendencies because he has minimized them in himself and can now criticize them in others. It is safe for him to get angry at these qualities because they do not belong to him but to another. In this way, different groups within the Church can accuse each other of bad faith or unwillingness to dialogue when this is really their own problem. If they can make the accusation against the other they can be properly indignant and can also excuse themselves from further relationship with the other. Projection is a favorite device of the preacher who handles his own difficulties by accusing the congregation of possessing them. The sign of this is always the exaggerated measure in which these ills are attributed to others. It is a very functional defense because it eliminates the need to face oneself fully or to work at establishing better relationships with others.

Closely allied to this is the defense of *reaction-formation* in which an individual can hide a motive of his own by expressing in very strong terms exactly the opposite feeling. This is seen, for example, in the mother who is threatened when her idea of herself as a good mother is challenged by feelings of not wanting or caring much for one of her children. Reaction-formation is evident when she defends herself against these feelings by expressing excessive attention or affection for the child in question. Overprotective parents are frequently protecting only themselves when they lavish attention on their children. This reduces the anxiety they would experience if they had to face and work through their real feelings about such a situation.

Reaction-formation is evident in the Church in those crusaders who protest too much. It is clear, for example, in the critics of celibacy who speak just a little too loudly about their masculine needs. If they are sure of their sexual identity, they hardly need to be defensive about it. On the other hand, reaction-formation is also used by crusaders, especially regarding purity, who betray their own uneasiness about sexuality by their exaggerated campaigns for modesty. This is not to say that anyone in favor of modesty is necessarily defensive. It is clear, nonetheless, that many crusaders are very uneasy about the subject of their crusade. The incredible detail, the almost sick curiosity they have about women's bodies and the clothing that adorns them, betray their own difficulty.

Reaction-formation is frequently the inspiration of the censor who likes to ban books and would, if it were at all fashionable, burn them publicly. He is dealing with a problem of his own, rather than with a true social ill. His campaign is forceful because it thereby fights his own fascination for the subject of it.

Reaction-formation probably shows itself best in the heightened self-righteousness that characterizes the pronouncements of churchmen on sexuality. This was clear in the aftermath of the encyclical *Humanae Vitae*. All out of proportion to the way prelates had followed up previous encyclicals was the uneven and intemperate reaction of those who wanted to make the test of faithfulness to Church rest solely on the resolute acceptance of this document. Their excessive language and pessimistic view of man made evident to the world that they had not dealt very effectively with their own sexuality. There is no subject on which a preacher can wax more eloquent than sexual sin. This did not seem to be the attitude of Christ as far as one can judge from reading the Gospels. The irate churchman, when he shouts about sex, tells more about himself than anything else. Again, it is the exaggerated quality of the attack which indicates that it is defensive in nature. Not all crusaders or reformers are so motivated when they authentically strive for reform. They see things in proportion and their feelings are in much better balance.

Dissociation is a defense in which there is a split between the actions, emotions, and thinking of an individual. Dissociation indicates a splitting within the person and it can show itself in many forms. Common manifestations of this defense are compulsive actions and excessive theorizing.

Compulsive actions are sometimes actually substituted for authentic religious behavior. Indeed, in the days when the guilt machine was operating well, compulsive acts were resorted to by individuals who thereby shielded themselves from feelings of guilt. Compulsive actions substitute for an individual's full facing of himself in order to integrate all the aspects of his behavior. When religion is taught in stark terms, and when people are not told the complete truth, they sometimes can only use compulsive acts to quiet their anxiety. This largely explains the phenomenon of scrupulosity which showed itself through the repetition of prayers or the carrying out of certain religious actions in a forced and uneasy way. Compulsive activity frequently masks strong feelings of anger which would come to the surface if the person did not have this defense mechanism handy.

The prayer life of the Church took on the nature of compulsive activity in many of its manifestations. The sign of this defense is the automatic quality with which the actions or the words are carried out or spoken. That is why the recitation of the office, the rosary, or the Mass could be rushed through with a minimal atmosphere of prayer about it. The deed was done, the anxiety had been avoided, and the person was free to go about his business. It was this kind of defense which led people to speak about the divine office or other prayers or spiritual exercises in terms of "getting it in." It is this kind of defense which is deaf to the real spirit of prayer or devotion. It was somehow acceptable because it quieted anxiety through conveying the feelings that solemn obligations had been carried out.

An illusion of accomplishment went along with a whole range of compulsive Catholic behaviors. That is precisely why it is so threatening for many people to find that these previously effective tactics are being questioned at the present time. A person felt better, in other words, if he rushed through his office mindlessly because it reduced his anxiety about his obligation to say it under the pain of mortal sin. He had done what was demanded of him if he were to see himself as good. So it also was with the attendance at Mass or the recitation of many other prayers. Once they were said, a supposedly good deed had been accomplished. Now, however, people wonder about the genuineness of such kind of prayers. They ask openly whether they ever had much value. This is threatening because it takes away the mechanism which tamed anxiety in the past. The search for an authentic prayer life is sometimes ridiculed by defensive persons who prized so highly the automatic recitation of prayers or the automatic performance of the liturgy in a past era. If a new generation which questions these practices is right, then they must re-examine the sincerity of their whole prayer life. This is indeed a very threatening kind of challenge. Consequently there is very strong feeling connected with what seem to be such minor and sensible adjustments in Christian behavior. People are tampering with defenses which were highly ritualistic and not really satisfying for the maturely religious person.

They were, however, very satisfying for those who did not want to confront themselves about their need for compulsive religious practices.

Dissociation can also manifest itself through excessive theorizing. This latter process substitutes talking or thinking about something for really doing something about it. The longer an individual can talk, the less anxious he is about facing the challenge of life itself. There is no shortage of discussion groups or of beautiful sermons about Christian love although it seems to be hard to come by in the ordinary life of the Church. Excessive theorizing or intellectualization is the classic defense of the person who is basically incapable of action. It appears in the Church whenever the great talk about principles is not matched in the world of activity. In the post-conciliar era it is indeed fascinating to talk about the themes of Vatican II. It is a much more difficult business to reduce these to action. The defense is employed, then, to forestall action on the part of those who are not really ready to commit themselves to the Christian life. They talk, and then they talk some more, or perhaps they hold a symposium. Not all of these things are defensive, obviously, but enough of them are to suggest that we might confront ourselves about some of our high-flown "dialogue" and its relationship to our actions with a little more severity in the future.

Repression, unconscious in nature, is a classic form of defense by which impulses, tendencies, or wishes are kept in check by denying them publicly. This is to deny human nature and to attempt to maintain a picture of oneself that is more angelic than fleshy. Repression does not allow an individual to face the fullness of this humanity. As a result he does not deal constructively with it. Repression differs from suppression in that the latter is a conscious process. This is used often enough in the Church as well. There are things that a person is not supposed to talk about or to bring up in polite company. He will be thought the less of if he does. That is the fate of people who want to point out difficulties, whether they be about infallibility or the nature of married life. These kind of people, their writings and their speeches, can be and are suppressed. As the old Turkish proverb has it, "The man who tells the truth should have one foot in the stirrup."

Repression, however, finds the person unaware of the phenomenon which he is repressing. It is therefore much more difficult to deal with and requires much more openness to the self if one is to discover the source of the difficulty. The main problem with either of these techniques of defense is that they are not successful. Nothing is ever put completely out of mind. The impulses which are pushed down tend to express themselves indirectly. Repression is served by many of the defense mechanisms which have just been discussed. They serve repression because they allow the expression of forbidden impulses in disguised forms which are mislabeled so that the person can maintain a better picture of himself.

In the Church, this is common in the area of sexual behavior. Nothing has been disguised more and talked about with less lucidity than the sexual impulses of man. These are very varied. If one does not face them directly they will assert themselves anyway. This is evident in the grotesque distortions that have emerged in the lives of people who have refused to deal directly with their sexual feelings. It is a sad and difficult truth, one which we will discuss later on in this book, and it probably represents one of the areas which could most benefit from the light of truth.

These are some of the classic defenses that one can see expressed in the Church at this time. The defenses work well for a little while but, in the long run, they betray the individual or the institution which uses them. In fact, some of the turmoil of the contemporary Church arises precisely because of the defensive bent of those who have been afraid to face the truth. It is this style of defense, through denial or disguise, which must be confronted if renewal is to proceed on a sound basis. Defenses are really only put aside if people are willing to love each other enough to accept each other's imperfections and failings. It is the truth, and the truth alone, that will make the Church free.

The Theology of Caution

The cautious and tentative approach of Church leaders to the renewal of the institutions of the Church is a logical result of a basically defensive attitude toward life. Caution is the strategy of choice for the man on guard who feels that something he possesses is in danger. Renewal endangers the ecclesial forms which are so familiar to religious leaders. It seems quite clear that they are committed to the preservation of these structures or, at most, to a minimal reworking of them. Again, this is to mistake institutional patterns for the essence of Christianity. It is difficult to deny that defensive churchmen operate on this principle.

They do not necessarily take this position consciously. It comes automatically from establishment habit. Few churchmen would with full awareness say that they put priority on institutions before people. They are more likely to say that the institutions are for the service of the people, that the institutions represent an evolutionary embodiment of Christian life and practice, and that to allow them to be transformed would threaten the very existence of organized religion. In other words, in an army-like style, Church leadership reacts to maintain the institution for what it conceives to be the best of reasons. It does not allow itself the opportunity to study these institutions deeply and to find out whether they can still serve mankind effectively or not. The important thing, as they see it, is to hold the thing together. While doing this they do not allow themselves to take a look at the human cost and suffering that follows from this position.

When one takes the position that most supports the institution, one also chooses the position which is the most severe on human beings. There is a tension between the individual and the institution. If one elects to reinforce the institution, then one automatically places the individual in second, and in this case, last, place. That is the only reason that can explain the traditionally slow process of dealing with urgent and painful human problems. Marriage cases are a good example. The individuals must wait, often in the most agonizing circumstances, while the mills of ecclesiastical bureaucracy grind their decrees exceeding fine. Many defend this style, claiming that its slow and deliberate pace ensures that individuals do not make any decisions impulsively. Granting the need for cooling-off periods in human affairs, the unhurried rate at which the Church transacts business is still excessive. With the notable exception of American and Canadian canon lawyers, no one seems ever to have challenged seriously the long-accepted myth that the Church must do things slowly and therefore wisely. This procedure has clearly served the institutional forms well over the centuries.

The style of the institution, a majestic and serene otherworldliness, enabled it to calculate problems according to eternal values. That style is my candidate for the most elaborate defense mechanism ever devised by churchmen. There is no valid reason why intelligent men, aided by the Spirit and grounded in good theology, cannot handle human problems, such as marriage cases, with quite reasonable dispatch. Perhaps their own pattern of life would be disrupted if ecclesiastics cleared their court calendars, as many observers have suggested they could do in rather short order. In other words, the sluggardly pace of ecclesiastical courts may meet the needs of the judges and the institution far more than it does the needs of the Christians who are sincere and honest enough to present their case to the court in the first place.

The seeming reluctance to adjudicate marriage cases extends also to the process of laicization for priests and dispensations for members of religious orders. It is not bad enough that the people who seek these may be treated to indignities of inquiry which they hardly deserve. They are then customarily subjected to a wait, the length of which is difficult to predict for any particular case. All of these people, whether they seek a decision about their marriage or about their status in the priesthood or religious life, must be presumed to be in good faith. Characteristically they have searched themselves and come to a painful and difficult decision. Most of them are not gay divorcees or mindless deserters from a good cause. They are simple, down-to-earth people who have made mistakes. Now, in accordance with the laws of their Church, they seek to rectify these and to begin their lives anew.

The ecclesiastical mind thinks that if you make it too easy for people to get out of previously contracted obligations, you will weaken the overall discipline of the institution and encourage other people to make the same kind of move. This is exactly the fear which motivates some of the slowness that has clearly been present in dealing with these types of cases. Again, it is the tactic of those whose main commitment is to a rigid institutional form and who react negatively to anything that seems to threaten this. They maintain that the Church will fall apart if it does not strictly enforce its rules and regulations. It falls apart far more rapidly when it abandons compassion, understanding, and a sense of justice in dealing with people. These are precisely the values, however, which are underplayed when the first defensive concern is to preserve this structure and its discipline. While it may strengthen some sort of institutional stability, it also exacts a fearful toll from the suffering human beings who are made to wait while the clock keeps counting the days of their lives away.

Because of the typical patterns of delay some sympathetic chancery officials have begun to operate in relationship to people outside the ordinary lines for dispensations and other documents from higher authorities. They have faced the facts with individuals that, although their case for annulment or some other decision is valid, the time it would take to get an answer makes another approach a better Christian possibility for them. They ignore the traditional ecclesiastical procedures, telling people to keep it quiet, and send them back to their own lives without having involved them in the fatiguing and perhaps ultimately frustrating court process. These officials are not trying to tear the Church down. They are merely making an effort to be understanding of the human condition as they carry out their function of service. They understand that their service is for the people. It is with regret that they see institutional forms as impediments, but they are no longer afraid to take short cuts which they believe God will understand. This is exactly the kind of harvest that the institutional

Church, so bent on preserving its forms and discipline, reaps while it deludes itself about the wisdom of its slow-paced procedures. In other words, insistence on rigid tactics ultimately disrupts rather than strengthens administrative structures.

As long as institutional-minded churchmen are not ready to deal forthrightly with the problems of marriage they will continue the style of ecclesiastical justice that has just been described. Many of the men most sensitive to the antiquated nature of Church machinery have already seen too much suffering in the lives of the petitioners who come before them. These members of ecclesiastical courts have preserved priestly hearts even though they have had to serve the Church as legal minds. Some of these men have courageously pointed out the difficulties and have suggested that it is time for the Church to restudy all its procedures in connection with marriage cases. These men often meet their ecclesiastical fate quickly and surely. Monsignor Stephen Kelleher, with twenty-five years of experience, raised serious questions about marriage court procedure in an article in *America* and was quickly retired a few weeks after it was published. Men like Monsignor Kelleher are prophets, however, who remind the Church that it is fundamentally to be of service to its people and that it must be ready to risk everything in order to carry out that mission.

This is a dangerous kind of confrontation for a member of the establishment to put forth. It is in the way that men like Monsignor Kelleher are treated that the cold and defensive qualities of decayed institutionalism make themselves most manifest. He was treated the way an insubordinate officer would have been treated in one of the armed services. He was treated after the fashion of a political machine punishing some party members who had not voted according to the party line. Party machines and military life must maintain the discipline of their members at all costs. That is the essence of their institutional character. Even these realms have been badly shaken in recent years. That the Church should find itself employing the same tactics is a terrible reminder of its touchy defensiveness. This kind of caution challenges the credibility of the Church as a transcendent institution which has a sense of what is beyond life. It is, however, a logical extension of the defensive posture which automatically adopts the most conservative positions to preserve itself.

Some churchmen obviously do not realize that their defensiveness has raised questions of conscience in the minds of many other members of the Church. These latter have found themselves, quite unexpectedly, in a position in which the weight of the institution has been placed hard against them in order to get a conforming response out of them. This may represent some ecclesiastical desire to close ranks quickly when disputed questions arise. It is not at all an easy situation for sincere Christians whose own integrity could be compromised by some kind of blind and bowing deference to the wishes of uneasy ecclesiastical authorities. The reactions to the papal encyclical *Humanae Vitae* are a good example of this. The Holy Father obviously took the most conservative stand possible even though he made clear his knowledge of new discoveries and understandings in the physical and social sciences. He did not make it his task to integrate this new knowledge with the traditional teaching of the Church, preferring to reiterate the teaching which had been held for such a long time. This stand, which defended the past, did indeed aim at preserving institutional continuity and institutional form.

The manner of presenting the encyclical by the now Archbishop Lambruschini, whose elevation to the episcopate may mark a further similarity between the Church and the army, did not help things. He spoke of further research which might lead the Church to "launch contraception." No one was quite sure for a while exactly what had happened since this initial communication was so confusing.

This was quickly settled, however, by the ecclesiastics who chose to fight it out on the line of *Humanae Vitae* if it took them all summer. It ended up taking them far beyond that season into a winter of deep discontent. Their purpose was clearly to preserve the teaching authority of the Church. They reacted testily and with authoritarian dispatch against those who said that despite the papal document, questions in their own conscience still remained unresolved. This defensive blunder on the part of certain Church leaders betrayed the fact that they were not trying to understand the questions concerning birth regulation as much as they were putting all their energies into trimming the ark for its continued well-disciplined voyage through salvation history. It is to the credit of many other ecclesiastical leaders that they avoided this collision course with their priests or people. Where it did take place, however, it was public and painful enough to do great damage both to people and to the institution itself.

The worst part of the whole situation is the shabby service it has done to men of integrity who are trying to think through the problem, not merely for their own benefit, but in light of its implications for the whole human race. These include priests and lay people, but especially the Catholic scientist who is well acquainted with the advances in the understanding of man which have taken place during the twentieth century. As one example, I think of the many fine Catholic psychologists and psychiatrists with no wish to be disloyal to the Church or to the Pope who could not equate the pronouncements of the encyclical with what they know about man from their disciplines. They found the encyclical inconsistent and dependent upon a fragmentary and outdated psychology of man. They found it full of assertions about the psychological effects of contraception which were not supported by proof. For example, the encyclical claims that the use of birth regulation methods will lower the status of women and will lead to immorality. For these men the issuance of the encyclical and the subsequent demand by certain ecclesiastics for absolute loyalty to its teaching, created a crisis in conscience. The Holy Father and the Church did not integrate the findings of research and the understanding of scientific principles into the reasoning or decisions of the encyclical.

These men have been asked to accept a decision based on arguments in which they have no faith. This is not to say that they lack faith in the Pope or the Church. It is to place them in a very difficult position and to leave them unaided by any sign of understanding of their difficulty, either in the encyclical itself or on the part of ecclesiastical observers and interpreters. This dilemma of conscience is real, not only for scientists but for thousands of other people of good will. It is a classic example of how a cautious approach, afraid to acknowledge the development of thought or to integrate it into Church teaching, causes tremendous suffering for sincere people. Worse still, the Church did not seem able or willing to respond to the intellectual difficulties of these people. Many compassionate and understanding statements have been made. Most of these have been made in view of what has been described as the weakness of human nature. The tragedy is that no response has been directed effectively at one of the strengths of human nature, the thinking mind. The cautionary approach rules this out. While it can be forgiving of sinners, it fails to address itself to the deep intellectual needs of modern man.

This whole situation has raised any number of issues. It demonstrates the need for institutional reform far more than it preserves institutional structure. In other words, quite the reverse of what had been hoped for is really occurring. People still remember Galileo or, more recently, the needlessly absolute and regressive biblical decrees which for more than a generation caused such embarrassment and stagnation for Catholic scholars. They are not of a mind to submit themselves to this kind of process again. They feel more akin to Magellan who once said, "The Church says the earth is flat; but I have seen its shadow on the moon and I have more confidence even in the shadow than in the Church." The intellectual needs of men have not been met by the supercautionary approach of *Humanae Vitae* which, quite aside from its statement on birth regulation, proved so disappointing to mature and thinking individuals.

The cautious approach, which fails to deal with the latest scientific discoveries and intellectual understandings, alienates those people who should be a source of the Church's informing itself about current questions. The Church learns through the experience of the Christian community under the action of the Spirit. If it cannot make room for the wisdom of the Christian community then it has cut off one of its chief sources of intellectual growth. Indeed, for too many centuries thinkers have been automatically suspect by the watchdogs of orthodoxy. The Church has not always provided a cordial and encouraging atmosphere for their scholarly pursuits. It has been frankly skeptical and intolerant of new ideas. Its style, in fact, is to catch up with intellectual movements at least a generation after the rest of the world has responded to them. The Church ends up dealing with what is no longer new just when the rest of the world is moving on to a new frontier.

The cautious nonintellectualism of the Church demonstrates the way churchmen can so wed themselves to the opinions of ages that are passing away. It is characteristic of them to give themselves over to the ebbing tides of thought because they are afraid even to look in the direction of swift new currents. This is the tragic aftermath of an ecclesiastical stance which has long outlived its usefulness. Aimed at institutional self-preservation, it is not successful even in accomplishing this any more. Excessively cautious people are unable to relate in a stable way either to themselves or to others. Caution finally trips them up because others are never quite sure what they are trying to say. This leads them to misjudge the cautious individual and perhaps to misinterpret him. All the cautions become undone through the excessive insistence on this procedure. This was typified, for example, in national politics, by the statements of the secretary designate of the treasury, David Kennedy, shortly after his nomination. Striving to be cautious about the price of gold and, as he put it, "to keep his options open," he was badly misunderstood and there was a run on the price of gold the very next day.

In the Church, this approach has been given the somewhat exalted name of prudence. Prudence, however, is that virtue which concerns itself with the choice of the proper means to achieve lawful ends. It is difficult to construe nonactivity as a healthy means to any kind of end. The Church has given itself a great name for making haste slowly. It is really time that we confronted the fact that this is a defensive rationalization for not being able to deal with the pace and character of the world around us. In a turbulent environment, this kind of posture is as intolerable as it is ineffective. It fails in preserving the institutional structure of the past while at the same time it causes untold anguish in the lives of millions of its people. It causes bewilderment and frustration and unnecessary crises of conscience.

Supercaution, christened prudence, reveals the arthritic condition of the institution which still wants to measure itself in inches in a universe that is concerned with light years. This style makes it clear that the Church is not able to reveal a consistent identity to the world. It makes it difficult for the Church to establish firm and helping relationships to mankind because men are never sure of what the Church's attitude, as expressed by churchmen, really is. The Church seems unable to relate to the sciences, except in a somewhat patronizing if vaguely encouraging way. The theology of caution underscores the inability of churchmen to incorporate new learning and new discoveries into the Church's understanding of the world it is called to serve. A favorite device of a cautionary churchman over the generations, for example, has been to look at new discoveries and, for some reason or other, to write long treatises on whether they are acceptable according to traditional Christian doctrine. This is very different from trying to learn from or with these men. It is to make medieval categories the measure of all new learning. This is one of the roots of the caution which has so disastrously undone itself in our own day.

Such caution can only arise in response to fear. But what is there to be afraid of? If the authority of the Church is so secure, then it hardly needs to defend itself constantly and petulantly against any questions which may arise in the course of history. It seems clear that churchmen are unsure of the dimensions of their own authority, or the manner in which it should be exercised. Defensive Church leaders continue to misidentify transient ecclesiastical forms with the eternal and essential truths which Christ speaks to mankind. Some churchmen seem to have very little faith in Christ's promises of His abiding presence when they betray their own plaguing lack of confidence in good Christian people. The problem is clearly theirs, not their people's. Otherwise the curia would fight for truth rather than make itself over into some Vatican Committee on Un-Roman Affairs. Caution simply does not work any more. This merely illustrates the need to re-examine and restyle the patterns of Church structure in the modern world. The problem which plagues administratively oriented churchmen is that they lack sufficient faith in the institutional evolution which is the sign of the vigorous Church that is just coming into being. It is faith in the growth of a Church where all things are indeed made new that they must exhibit at this time. The structures must be changed so that the Church can once again give itself fully in service to its people. It can then live with the Gospel peace of mind that Christ will preserve it as long as it is true to this challenge.

Ex-Priests without Tears

Symptomatic of the changes going on in the Catholic Church at the present time is the increasing number of persons who are withdrawing from the priesthood and the religious life. While this phenomenon has been variously interpreted, it can be related to the deep need of the institutional Church to restructure itself. This includes the manner and the conditions of life for the priests, brothers, and sisters who constitute the service personnel for the People of God. Both the priesthood and religious life have undergone reformulation in past eras. It is not surprising to find this challenge arise again. Virtually all the major professions are now redefining their manner of response to the needs of the world. It is true that departure from the priesthood or religious life is a radical solution for individual persons. It points, however, to a more profound problem to which Church leaders have not as yet given their full attention.

During the era when the institution of the priesthood and religious life went unquestioned within the overall organization of the Catholic Church, the resigned priest was typically regarded as a tragic figure, for whom there could yet be redemption through some final heroism. This was typified in the motion picture *Titanic* in which the unfrocked priest donned his stole and descended "for God's sake" into the exploding boiler room. So tight-knit was the priestly class to which he belonged, so absolute the condemnation should he leave it, so reprehensible was he in the eyes of his family and fellow Catholics, that he was generally considered a failure. The ideal solution to his difficulty in the minds of his superiors and fellow priests was the unquestioned notion that they should do everything to "get him back" into the priesthood. Great fraternal concern was exhibited in trying to achieve this goal for the man who had left the service of the Church. This was frequently accompanied by placing the blame for the resignation of the individual on some seductive woman who had tempted him into a lesser kind of life. Prayers were offered for the "defector" but there remained a pretty grim if seldom-employed ceremony of defrocking which was not unlike the ritual ripping off of the disgraced soldier's epaulets. Resigned priests disappeared into society except for those very few who turned their recollections of the priesthood into some form of commercial profit through writing or lecturing.

On the other side, recent years have seen some former priests proclaim themselves as heroes and prophets who have been brave enough to denounce the Church and to get themselves out of it. They see no meaning or possibility of service in any organized religion or organized priesthood. Some of these men have, in fact, written and spoken with a great deal of hostility. They have received a certain amount of celebration in some quarters and they have received a great deal more publicity than was the case with any of their predecessors.

Some of these former priests, of course, have mistaken rudeness for speaking the truth. The majority of them, however, have left the priesthood quietly in search of a new life. Many of these are reflective men who have made a painful decision with no interest in causing any dramatic scene.

The number of resignations from the priesthood and religious life is now increasing within the Catholic Church. There is no sign that this trend is stopping or even leveling off. It constitutes a major problem to which Church leaders must give not only prayerful concern but also a measure of analytic study. The problems of ex-priests have not as yet received any thorough investigation through the application of scientific research. The bishops of the United States authorized a study in depth of the life and ministry of the priest in 1967. But as 1969 dawned they had just signed the long-prepared contracts to carry this out. In the absence of any research answers as yet, it is important to review and to try to understand the meaning of this phenomenon.

What have been the reactions on the part of the Church to these priests and religious who have left its service? In the first instance, as a self-preserving institution, the Church moves to protect itself by making it difficult and even shameful for men to leave the priesthood. This was a powerfully functional approach, especially when the guilt machine was working efficiently in the years before the Second Vatican Council. Just as court-martials and the threat of dishonorable discharges maintained discipline in the armed forces, so the uncomfortable treatment waiting for the priest who contemplated resignation served as a powerful deterrent to his carrying it through. It was always possible for priests to seek laicization, that is, to return to the state of the layman in exchange for giving up their right to function as priests. The permission to marry never went along with this decree. The ex-priest, while no longer bound to serve within the Church, was obliged to remain celibate and, at times, even to recite the daily office. Should he marry, he would incur further ecclesiastical penalties and be told by the Church that his marriage was not a valid one in its eyes.

Vatican II saw the beginning of a shift in this policy. An effort was made, as it was somewhat ungraciously described, to "fix up" the marriages that had been contracted by former priests. For a period of time it was necessary for a man to marry outside the Church after he had received his decree of laicization before the Church machinery could deal with the regularization of his married state. This was, in simple fact, an agonizing problem for the ex-priest who felt that he had to commit the sin of marrying outside the Church before he could get any consideration from the Church which would allow him once more to receive its sacraments in good faith.

This extremely punishing procedure clearly aimed at supporting the institutional structures of the priesthood within the Church. It made resignation from the priesthood a very difficult and searing personal experience. This has changed at the present time, and men who choose to leave the priesthood can receive a dispensation to marry at the time they resign. This process, however, may be very lengthy and may involve a number of investigations before it is carried through. I have known many priests who have waited more than a year for action on their petitions for laicization. It is, nonetheless, a step forward from the previous practice which could hardly be described as gentle and humane treatment. In fact, the resigning priest frequently was subjected to lectures from his superior or bishop who felt that he was committed to holding firm the ranks as strictly as possible.

I recall well a priest who had prayed and thought about his decision for several months before approaching his bishop. He was convinced that, although it was painful to do it, leaving the priesthood was the right thing for him. His bishop received him coldly at this crucial moment, told him that he was an "Indian giver" who had broken his promises to God and was doing a quite dishonorable thing. Not all bishops and superiors so address themselves to the priests who leave their service, but it is not an isolated occurrence. One example of this kind of treatment, in the minds of many, would be one too many for leaders who are supposed to be sensitive and understanding of human difficulties. It is, as has been noted, the kind of response that serves the institution by making it so exceedingly difficult to separate oneself from it in good grace. It is a good thing that these tactics have come to light even though this has occurred bitterly and with great resentment at times.

Now that the guilt machine has broken down, the stigma attached to leaving the priesthood is considerably less than it was. Indeed, the improved practice of granting permission to marry suggests that many bishops are aware of the enormous burdens which the administrative regulations of the Church have placed on ex-priests. They have tried to do something about it. The Catholic people, whose record for understanding and forgiving their clergy is probably without parallel in the history of the world, have seen enough of life not to be scandalized by a man who chooses to change the direction of his career. Priests and religious feel more free, in other words, to make decisions whose former built-in penalties have been considerably diminished. Even with this change of tone, however, there are ecclesiastics whose commitment to the institution is so great that they cannot classify these men or women as anything but deserters from the cause. "Traitor" is not too strong a word for them to employ, because they feel that those who leave the priesthood weaken it as a group and tend to eat away at the foundations of the Church's structure. They have a need to brand these men in this fashion or it would be very difficult for them to live with the phenomenon at all.

Perhaps the most familiar description of the departing priest says he never belonged in the priesthood in the first place or that he was a psychological misfit. This clarity of hindsight supports the structure of the priesthood by making those who leave it misguided and errant individuals. This protects the Church from really re-examining the structures of the priesthood to see if these might not be somehow at fault in contributing to the decision of a man to withdraw. This kind of reasoning was at least partially present in Pope Paul VI's encyclical on celibacy issued in June, 1967. He called for more careful examination of candidates, even for the use of psychological testing to keep out of the priesthood the kind of men who had recently left it. This, of course, oversimplified the problem inasmuch as it regarded most ex-priests as sick and undeveloped personalities. This is also typical of the Church's late-breaking interest in scientific approaches. It had seldom endorsed psychological testing with any enthusiasm during the previous twenty years.

This raises, according to many observers, the question of whether the measure of a man's fitness for serving the Church can adequately be summed up in whether he can lead a celibate life or not. This criterion of aptitude leaves out many dimensions of personality which may be vitally important in a person who wishes to dedicate his life in religious ministry to others. The question was clearly not settled by the papal encyclical. It tended to deal in abstract and ideal terms about a question whose insistent pressure has risen steadily ever since. Again, however, it expressed the attitude of those unwilling to investigate the nature and conditions of life in the priesthood thoroughly. If there is no flaw in the institutional forms of the priesthood, then the blame can easily be placed elsewhere for the crescendoing problems of adjustment that are apparent within the ranks of priests and religious throughout the world. This is an excellent example of an area where men have been unwilling to search out the truth because it might threaten long-established traditions.

If one approaches former priests and religious as individuals it is difficult to find many who seem either like brazen rebels or terribly wayward people. They seem rather like ordinary men and women who have had to work through an extraordinarily difficult decision, usually after much pain and much prayer. They are intelligent, mild-mannered, and somewhat lost in trying to find a new life in a larger world. Most of them move into occupations which are oriented to the service of people, such as teaching, social work, or various positions in governmental programs like the Office of Economic Opportunity. Often these former priests, sisters, and brothers cluster together in mutual support groups. This is especially true in the larger cities in the United States, to which they often make their way after leaving their communities or their dioceses. The larger cities offer a certain anonymity, a fresh setting after a sharp turn in the direction of their lives. Former priests and religious are no longer without some organized assistance in their readjustment. Groups such as "Bearings," founded and largely staffed by former priests or religious, have offices in the larger cities which offer counsel, companionship, and help in securing new jobs.

Some note that it is only the ex-priest or religious who finds an organization prepared to assist him in changing the pattern of his life and occupation. This is afforded to very few other groups in our culture, most of whom find themselves on their own in establishing a new life. It is also true, however, that few groups are as unprepared for this change-over as are priests and religious. Many of them, because of the college seminaries or novitiates which they attended, do not have academic degrees which are recognized in the secular world. They have been prepared in subjects and skills which are not always easily translatable into paying jobs. Many of the former priests and religious realize this difficulty, even as they acknowledge that no other occupation gives people the luxury to think over and prepare for a major change in quite the way that the priesthood or religious life does. In the service of the Church, however, they have had the time and the freedom from dependents to contemplate and to plan to some extent for a radical reorientation of their lives. Men and women with families to support or other relationships to sustain may have to stick at their unappetizing occupation out of sheer necessity. There are mouths to feed and children to get through college. This is not true for the former priest and religious who, if they are unprepared for the outside world, are also freed from the limiting demands of family life in changing their career.

What they do give up, when they finally reach their decisions, are security, familiar surroundings, and the rewards of respect and approbation from the institution and the people they serve. For many, it is very difficult to put these things aside and to test themselves in the marketplace of life's competition on their own merits. It is precisely because they feel they never have been tested in a realistic situation that some move out of the service of the Church. Their motivation is not easy to analyze, but it is clear that we must make every effort to understand it. One need not approve what they do to try to get a look at them as human beings. They are, as a group, no more heroic or cowardly than any other group in any other profession in life. Their sheer humanity and their struggles prompt us to try to view them with neither smirks nor tears.

I have dealt with scores of priests and religious in the throes of making the decision to withdraw from the Church. It was not easy for any of the ones that I knew. It is certainly true that some of them made a mistake when they first chose the priesthood or religious life. Many of these, however, were encouraged to remain with this vocational choice by teachers or superiors who had a very mistaken idea of what God expects from human beings. These superiors really did not give their subjects the freedom to make a decision during their years of training because, as they viewed it, the priesthood or the religious life was automatically better than anything else. Many of these priests and religious were never allowed to be free because the organizational dynamics of seminaries and other houses of training strongly reinforced the choice of service to the Church as God's unalterable will for them. An invitation from God could not be turned down, no matter how difficult or unappealing it might seem to the one who received it. This kind of advice, given all too often in the past, tended to bind these people psychologically to a way of life which they really did not examine in relationship to their own potential and their own needs. Some of them doggedly persevered even against the advice of some sympathetic elders who sensed that they would be unhappy. Why did they do this? Perhaps it was because they really wanted to serve other people, and, within the confines of Catholic life, the priesthood or sisterhood offered an enhancing opportunity and summit for doing this. It gave them status and, while it asked them to be poor, it also made them comfortable and secure.

Some of these priests are very intelligent men who had moved into religious orders that gave them the opportunity for intellectual development and expression through teaching in higher education. Characteristic of the training this kind of person received was a double bind of isolation from the world and its cares and a severe intellectualization of the processes of life. I have struggled in counseling with enough of these men to realize that it was only after they were ordained that they discovered that there were other aspects, both in life and in themselves, which they had never previously explored. They had never dealt, for example, with their emotional life or with their need for intimate companionship, and they had never had much experience in dealing with women. They got along acceptably in the gruff camaraderie of religious life. Many of them functioned very effectively as teachers. Sometime later, however, when the insulation of the life had been worn through by the strong winds of Vatican II, they awakened to another world around them. They no longer accepted everything, even the mistakes of the superior, as something God had foreordained for them for all eternity. They sensed their own personal needs and found these in conflict with the institution which allowed minimal freedom to them in their personal lives. It is not surprising to find deans and other university executives or chancery officials incapable of continuing within the organizational structure which permitted such little leeway to their overall personal development. Perhaps someone should have identified this difficulty at an earlier stage. This did not happen, mostly because the training period contributed to their over-intellectualized style of adjustment. It did not liberate them or help them to understand the fullness of their personalities. I do not want to make heroes out of the men who have had to face deep truths about themselves only in their mature years. I find it, however, understandable that they have had to grapple painfully with a decision about leaving the priesthood.

Another type of person whose pain I have shared in my office is the individual whose period of training and early experience in religious life was so controlled that it paralyzed the normal processes of personal development within him. Adolescence was suspended, and with it the tasks of learning to relate to authority, to the opposite sex, and to the achievement of his own personal identity. It comes as a shock to this person to find his adolescence reactivated when he is placed once again in relationship to people in a parish or students in a school. Sexual feelings that had been suppressed expressed themselves anew. Longings, which they had never allowed themselves to examine, come strongly into their hearts. They were truly strangers to themselves because for a long period in their life they were subjected to an organized kind of training which, in effect, put them in psychological incubation. In all honesty, at a later stage in life, they began to deal with these problems and found that they could no longer live within the confines of the priesthood or religious life.

Another type whose suffering I have witnessed is the priest or religious whose call to the Church came through a domineering parent, usually their mother. They always wanted to please their parents and to make them proud of them. They yielded to the wishes of a parent whose greatest pride would be realized in having a son or a daughter in the service of the Church. In great pain, this type of person comes to realize that his motivation was never his own, that, in fact, he had never dealt with his own interests or inclinations at all. He had wanted to please someone and, with the energies and enthusiasm of youth, he had followed through as best he could. With maturity, and with other life experiences, many of these have come to realize the shaky reasons which brought them to ordination or religious profession. It is true that many of them never really worked out their relationship to their parents very effectively. They were always the good boy or the good girl and they never moved beyond this. It is with grief and tears that they confront the controlling influence that one or the other parent has been on the whole course of their life. I have heard more than one, in contemplating his decision, speak of the people who would be hurt by the course of action he was about to choose. As one put it, "It will hurt my mother, it will probably kill her." In exploring this in therapy, one finds that this is exactly what this person wants to do by leaving the priesthood. It is not just the Church to which he is readjusting himself. It is to his original family as well. At last they are separating themselves from their parents, symbolically killing them through a decision which means liberation from their influence.

There are certainly many priests and religious who have had serious long-term emotional problems. To recognize this does not explain away the fact that they were accepted by their diocese or religious congregation and approved for service within the Church. It was only long afterward, perhaps after the extensive acting-out of alcoholism or sexual deviation, that these difficulties were recognized and that these people were considered unfit for the priesthood or religious life. It is not enough to dismiss them as sick, as though this excused us from examining the institutions of the Church. How could the institutions have made these kinds of mistakes? How could they have settled for candidates who had made no secret of their difficulties even during training periods only to receive reassurances that never quite worked out?

Mistakes are made, of course, in every profession. One should not be surprised to find that many have been made in the professions that serve the Church. What should be noted, however, is the prophetic quality of this phenomenon. Neurotic people, who desperately need the culture to remain stable around them, frequently tell us something about the future in the way they break down under stress. The neurotic or maladjusted individual senses the change in culture because he needs it to remain unchanged if he is to preserve his adjustment. It is not surprising to find many poorly adjusted people breaking down at this time in the history of the Church. They have sensed the changes in the general atmosphere which have occurred especially since the Vatican Council. They have been unable to cope with a shifting environment. One of the motives which brought them into the priesthood or religious life in the first place was that it seemed to offer such an unchanging environment in which to spend their lives. They are the first to find the collapsing conditions of community or rectory life impossible to accept. The first wave of people who left the priesthood found many of this type in their number. What is significant is that their experience has a message for the stronger and healthier members of their institutes or dioceses. The changed atmosphere in the Church has made these people sensitive to the structural weaknesses of the priesthood and religious life. The healthier people can tolerate these difficulties for a longer period of time. Sooner or later, however, they will experience the same difficulty. There is a prophecy in the neurotic breakdown, a prediction today of the kind of problem which the better adjusted members of the priesthood or religious life will probably have to face tomorrow.

This problem centers on the nature of institutionalized priestly and religious life. Even now, deeply sensitive men and women who honestly want to serve the Church are beginning to experience the strains which the breakdown of their neurotic colleagues predicted some time ago. There is a prophecy for the whole Church, then, in the way priests and religious are re-examining themselves in relationship to the styles of life which are supposed to support and express their service to God's people. A serious re-examination of the priesthood and religious life has been deferred and delayed by Church leaders, both men and women, who have accepted unquestioningly the traditional forms of priestly and religious life which are now so obviously showing structural fatigue.

This is not only a problem for the marginally adjusted personality. Healthy persons in the Church have been able to endure a great deal of stress and strain because of their inner strength. Now, however, the process of cultural change is so advanced that the healthy and sensitive person is particularly vulnerable. As Eugene Brody has observed (*American Journal of Psychiatry* 124:5, November 1967, "Trans-cultural Psychiatry, Human Similarities and Socioeconomic Evolution," p. 619):

> . . . regardless of social class distinctions, the poorly integrated community produced more psychiatric casualties than the well-integrated community. In other words, the most deprived individuals in a well-integrated community may be less psychiatrically vulnerable than more advantaged individuals in a disintegrating community.

This roughly describes the kind of psychological pressure under which the most sensitive and open personnel of the Catholic Church are now operating. The most able and understanding are exposed to the unique suffering that goes with understanding what is happening to them. They live at the precise point of conflict between old norms and new aspirations, in the open place between the disintegrated cultural model of the past and the as yet undesigned styles of life for the future. These people are often of deep faith and dynamic motivation. This tends to exacerbate the pain of conflict when they do not feel that there is yet enough flexibility or give in the institutional framework of the Church. They realize what must be done in the renewal of forms of service but they are discouraged at the overall insensitivity of Church bureaucracy. So this obvious challenge.

Since they are sensitive persons they have deep compassion for the human suffering that is inevitable at a time of culture break. They are hard-pressed at times to resolve their desire to respond to this suffering and their desire to be loyal to the Church authority which, casually and blindly, seems at times to cause the suffering. They feel the pressure in larger issues where loyalty to the Church and response to one's conscience seem to be counterpointed. They are sensitive about all discussions centering on the human person, his need for freedom, and his longings for substantial faith, hope, and love in his life. Their concern here only tightens the vise of their conflicted feelings when some segment of the Church seems to place institutional preservation ahead of these issues.

The best of the personnel are in this position because in a culture break men must search anew for the values by which they will live. These deep values are the ones that center on man rather than on his institutions. The sensitive clergyman reaffirms his belief in and need for basic human values at a time when the transforming institutional Church, intent on self-preservation, finds it difficult to incorporate these fully into its philosophy of personnel operation. That is why there will be continued tension around the personal aspects of the life of the Catholic priest and religious. And the one who will continue to suffer most is the sensitive, perceptive, and committed clergyman.

The experience of a rise in resignations from the priesthood and religious life cannot be written off merely as the actions of malcontents. It is just as unrealistic to make unblemished heroes of these people. Most of them do not desire this at all. The concern must be for a restructuring of the modes of service within the Church, not just to prevent resignations, but to make it possible for men and women to give their lives truly to the people who need their service so much. If Church leaders are unwilling to look at the deeper implications of these situations they can only preside over continued disintegration of forms of life that are quite clearly under severe stress at the present time. They owe this to the generations of priests and religious who want to serve God's people but who find their lives frustrated and painful because of the slow pace of institutional reform within the Church.

In the long run, it is the People of God who suffer from this inability of the Church leadership to deal effectively with this question. Former priests and nuns need neither condemnation nor condonation. They deserve understanding. So too do their brothers and sisters who have remained within the Church in hopes for the kind of reform that will revitalize their lives. Then they can refocus themselves on responding to the needs of those who are being served shabbily in the agonizing interim, the People of God who are the Church.

The Church for Man

The Church is for man. It is dangerously untrue to itself whenever it reverses this relationship in order to maintain a certain set of structures. The accidental and always changing forms of the Church literally do not have a life of their own. Whatever they are, from chancery offices to cathedral choirs, they are meant to serve the life of God's people. As such, they must never become so rigid that they are insensitive to the breath of the Spirit. When Church forms rigidify, the listing of the Spirit roars through the cracks like a killer hurricane. Only supple and flexible structures that reshape themselves under the impulse of the Spirit can serve as the sources of nourishment and life for men.

Churchmen commit themselves to persons as they are to help them become all that they can be through the action of the Spirit. They must affirm and encourage man the searcher, man the worker, and man the lover. In these vocations man finds the road to the fullness of his being. They are difficult vocations, these eminently human tasks of every life. Man's searching, his working, and his loving heal his wounds of sin and estrangement because through these he discovers and expresses the meaning of his life. The Church recognizes man in these tasks and strengthens and directs him to accomplish them through its teaching and sacraments. The Church as a people constitute the pilgrim presence of support and encouragement in which men share friendship in the Spirit.

It is clear that the Church cannot serve man if he is treated as something other than man. He is neither pure spirit nor pure animal. Misunderstandings about the nature of man always cause the Church to deal with him inappropriately. Unfortunately, there have been tragic mistakes in this regard during the course of history. Man treated as an angel is not man at all. On the other hand, many churchmen have viewed him less as a man and more as an animal, even though a noble and daring one. Seen this way, man needs to be broken, branded, and kept restrained from running wild. But man is not this either. Nor is he an animated marionette to be manipulated by master puppeteers of higher wisdom and responsibility. It is small wonder that those with distorted views of man have failed to help him grow to the maturity which is proper to the human condition. Any service to man which does not help him to become more of a man is a disservice to him.

The task of the Church is to make man more human, more conscious of his destiny and the conditions of his pilgrimage to eternal life. The Church must know what man is all about if it would help him to know what life is all about. Man cannot be led by force; he is moved, if at all, by the attractiveness of the Church's loving concern for him. The real power of growth is in the Gospels, which give man a direction and an understanding of his responsibilities. Man can only be understood as he is in the human condition, that quite remarkable unity of flesh and spirit who thinks and dreams, laughs and prays, and works and loves. The Church helps to make man whole or it has no hope of ever making him holy.

Everything in the Church should be ordered to this function of service or the Church has misunderstood its own nature and the nature of man as well. The Church, of all the world's institutions, should understand men deeply. It has survived with him and has known intimately his sinful failures as well as his visionary achievements. No other institution should feel more at home with man. No other institution should speak more clearly on his behalf. Indeed, if the Church does not defend man against those who would deform and manipulate him, if it does not fight for his rights and his dignity, no one else will do it.

Man's primary search is for himself. The Church's obligation, therefore, is to help man to understand and love himself. Churchmen must possess a deeply sensitive understanding of the person if they are to help men to recognize themselves in the universe that was made for their dominion. They must help men in the very process of living to plumb the depths of their own being, to get beneath the surface of life and to prize their existence. The Church stands by the side of man the searcher with compassion for his weakness as it presents to him the Christian ideal of his full humanity.

Man cannot search successfully unless the Church makes the light of the Spirit freely available to him. All Church forms, then, are really ordered to assist man in discovering himself and developing the communities of relationship which match his nature. Forms that are defended or preserved for their own sake may hinder rather than confirm man in his searching. The Church is a searcher too, always looking to reform itself so that it can effectively help man live the life of the Spirit. Churchmen cannot be surprised at their perennial need to fashion new forms of service to the human race. Man comes first, sinful man, man the wayfarer who needs God's help to become fully himself.

It has been a painful embarrassment for the Church when some of its members have set themselves against the search for a better understanding of man and his world. Most of this opposition has come from narrow minds which have clung tenaciously to rigid formulations of life. One hopes that the harrowing chapters of history which saw churchmen pitted against the advances of physical and social sciences are closed forever. Men like Galileo who looked beyond the horizons to see the world in the perspective of the universe were shamefully maltreated. So too, those like Freud who looked deeply into man were ridiculed, and their discoveries resisted until very recent times. To place oneself against truth is to sin against man the searcher and against the Holy Spirit as well.

Ordinary men search in far less dramatic ways as they make their way through life. They look for the meaning of their foibles and their insights. They look for better ways to work and live together. Nothing is a more magnificent characteristic of the person than his impulse to wonder about himself and his world. Indeed, man is healthy when he doubts and questions the formulations that no longer satisfy the facts which he observes. The Church cannot oppose itself to the creative strengths of the human race, although its past record in this regard has left a good deal to be desired. The Church, through Vatican II, is struggling to make a correction in its course and to catch again the tides and winds that carry man forward. With a compassion born of experience it can understand man the doubter and the questioner. It is safe for the Church to drop the defenses which made it suppress curiosity and wonder whenever these appeared. The self-satisfied mentality, exemplified in most of the question-boxes of Catholic papers, does not fit a Church that is supposed to help men find more of the truth all of the time. If the Church has been an awkward censor, it is now challenged to rediscover its own role as a tireless and undefensive searcher.

The Church helps man to enter into relationship with his world with a sense of reverence and responsibility for all of life. It presents this world to man in the perspective of the world to come. This view does not stigmatize this world as evil. The world is man's home, not his prison. The Church is meant to help human beings transform this world and to bring it to its fullness in relationship to its Creator. So it is not embarrassed by the world nor does it look on it as a drafty and unsuitable way station on the journey to heaven. It sees it much as God did in Genesis; it sees that it is good, and very good. Above all the Church helps man to enjoy life through entering into it vigorously here and now. The Church celebrates life because it understands it with the profound wisdom of God's inspiration and its own human experience.

The world is throbbing with the tortured search of oppressed men for freedom. It is no secret that the identification of the Church with the ways of monarchy has made it less than the leader in man's search for justice and freedom. American democracy was not enthusiastically endorsed by the authoritarian mentality of Rome. Yet the Church has grown vigorously in the environment of the United States whose Protestant Founding Fathers were at pains to separate Church from state. Through their efforts, the marriage of Church and government, one of the sources of the development of religious prejudice, was given a death blow. Some of the great figures of the American Church, Carroll, England, and Ireland, recognized this and gave their energies to the support of the American search for freedom. They were lonely voices, however, and a distant Roman home office was not always sympathetic to them. Indeed, "Americanism," the heresy that never was, was accorded the supreme distinction of being condemned.

In the continued turbulent search for freedom, men have wondered about the small participation of what is called the official Church. The energies for the support of minority groups have not come primarily from the Church. In fact, the ethnic groups which compose American Catholicism have been among the most strongly prejudiced in this regard. This may demonstrate the external character of their religious commitment, a phenomenon that was strengthened when being a good Catholic meant following the rules rather more than caring passionately for one's fellow man. So too, the Church has been remarkably silent during the last painful decade of American history. It has not joined its full energies as mediator in the terrible conflicts that have divided the country over civil rights, war, and the radicalization of the young. It is perhaps impossible to speculate about what the Church could have done to heal the American spirit during these years of riots and near-rebellion. It is clear, however, that it could have done more and that its absence mocked the fact that it should be a vital presence in these struggles. Long-winded and tedious pastoral letters, concern over internal affairs, a hesitant embarrassment about socially active Catholics—these are what we will regretfully remember as our part in man's search during the sixties.

The Church helps man to enter into relationship with God, not as some vague and unknowable force, but as He has revealed Himself through the incarnation and the Gospels. It is quite impossible for the Church to do this if it does not understand man. Without this, there is no understanding of the God who made Himself a servant for men by committing Himself to the human condition. The Church helps men to sense the world as a sign of God's existence and the setting for His ways with them. Churchmen must help men to pray, not in childish or magical ways, but in the mature dialogue of men who, understanding themselves, can open themselves to their Creator.

Man must be helped to worship in accord with his nature as he makes his offering of himself, his love and his work, back to God. Through the Church man is strengthened to transcend himself, to go beyond the limitations of the human condition through relationship with the God who is Love. In all this man can only be helped as man. He cannot be offered the prayers or forms of worship which fit pure spirits or driven animals. The tasks of prayer and worship can only mean something to man when the Church fits these to his proper psychological dispositions. The Church has bored man mightily with prayer and worship when it has tried to make him do these things in ways which did not suit his nature.

So too the Church understands work as intimately related to man's fulfillment. Its concern extends to everything that man fashions with his own energies. Work is man's share in the continuing miracle of creation.

He must have the decent conditions of freedom and fairness in which he can work with honor and dignity. The Church has fought for man's basic right to labor in a justly human way. This kind of battle never ends. The forces that would oppress man, whether of governments or technocracies, must always be confronted by the Church with the vision of man's inner dignity. The Church celebrates man the worker because it understands his labor as an essential expression of his personality. Man is not man unless he is able to invest his strengths and talents in creative activity. Through the constant understanding of the Church man has been encouraged to tame his environment, find the stars, and make the earth a peaceful home for himself. The Church blesses the arts and commerce, not as a mindless clerically-robed bystander, but with the intimate concern that challenges man to achieve his best performance in all his undertakings.

It is up to churchmen to look beyond labor in the setting of post-industrial society. Leisure and its proper use is already a pressing problem for countries like the United States. Apart from the observations of a few philosophers and theologians, the Church has not given much attention to this difficulty. It sighs reproachfully about man's flirtations with drugs and it stands as ready as ever to condemn his entertainments. These, however, are the signs of the times, the distractions, many quite empty and unfulfilling, to which man turns when affluence blesses him with more free time than he has ever known before. It is now important for churchmen to sense the changed order of things and to respond with a positive vision to guide man at play. With the "workingman's privilege" for Lenten fasting long since retired, the Church must reactivate a strength it has

allowed to grow stagnant, its imagination. Imagination
was not much needed in the era when the Church was
confident that it had the last word on all subjects of
human concern. Suddenly, however, in the face of ex-
panded leisure, it has little to say. The imagination is,
however, still there, waiting to be loosed again by churchmen who are aware of their responsibilities to the world.

Man is made to love, to share himself with others
always less selfishly. It is only with love that man can
really find what he searches for; it is only through love
that he can possess the full spirit of his creativity. With
love alone can man rest from his labors and enjoy his
world in the playfulness that flows unself-consciously
from full growth.

The Church possesses the most complete understanding of love that the world has ever known. This is found
in the Gospels and in the meaning of the life of Christ
Himself. Christ did not come so that men would multiply
the laws and codes of life. So the Church cannot imagine
that this is the way to help man to understand love.
Christ came to open man up through learning how to
die to himself so that he can reach out in life and love
to others. The essential Christian dynamic of loving has
never been supplanted. Above all other things, it is the
Church's business to respond to man's need to love and
be loved by others.

Love is learned in relationship to other persons and
it is always closely related to the willingness to die. The
ideal of the Christian who makes himself vulnerable
through reaching out in love to others retains an eternal
freshness and relevance. It is what man needs most to
understand. It is also what he gets most confused about,
especially when the Church fails to keep a real vision
of his human nature in mind as it deals with him. Life

is all about love and man's endless search for it. The Church strengthens man to love and to overcome the fear that makes him turn away from it. It tells him that he can never lose his beloved. This is the fundamental promise of the faith that springs from the Gospels. Men who open themselves to love embark on the most basic religious act of their lives. They join themselves by it to the redemptive flow of Christ's own life. Christ, after all, did not come to frighten men out of their wits or to give them detailed instructions on how to live. He told them that to be truly alive they had to love, that they had to expose themselves to the most risky enterprise men have ever perceived. If a man does not know how to love, he can never know much about the God who is love. St. John wrote that long ago, and yet for centuries churchmen have backed away from love because of their own fears about it.

This is a strange situation indeed. What is most important in life and what is most important in religion is an understanding of love. Without it an institution which calls itself religious reveals itself as an empty shell. Without it, men wither and harden so that they are hardly alive. It is the central experience of existence, the very essential point at which man discovers himself and God as well. Any Church that does not deal straightforwardly with love cannot really be of much help to man. It is not even much of an instrument for God. Like a matchbox house it is merely a structure of criss-crossed rules and pious notions in which no man can live. That is why churchmen who think their task is to control men are really never very much help to them. Their overemphasis on control puts love to death by destroying the freedom it needs to come alive.

Man really becomes a lover of God when he is able

to enter deeply into the meaning of human love. Unfortunately, many churchmen have made artificial distinctions about love that have caused a great deal of confusion. They have defined human and divine love over against each other, as competitors barely capable of coexistence. Yet all love comes from God. Man at his best lives the life that is given to him by God. That shows through in his least selfish and most glorious moments of loving others.

Love is something that fits man as he is. It is not something he does only with his mind. It flows from his total personality. It involves laughter and play and the joyous experience of sexuality. It is a pale image of itself when any of these human elements is ruled out or considered unworthy. When man truly loves he becomes fully himself. He is then united with God as he responds to the impulse of the Spirit who is the source of his power to love. Love transforms the lover as well as those he loves. Man hungers for sharing life with others. This opens him as nothing else does to share life with The Other who is God. If the Church cannot speak knowingly of love, if it cannot help men to learn to love a little better every day, then it fails at the only thing it really is called to do well.

At no time in history has it been more important for men to learn to love their enemies. It is much easier and strangely satisfying to what is immature in them to put them down. This man does through the raw explosion of primitive wells of violence or through the coldly cruel detachment of withdrawal. Someday men will be wise enough to acknowledge that they can kill each other in many ways. They put each other to death whenever they refuse to love, whenever they fail to root out the self-interest that closes them off from others. An

organized Church puts many people to death when it
can only deal with them defensively, strangling the life
out of them unconsciously because it can no longer open
itself in redemptive love to them. It closes the shutters
against hope and disillusions those who need faith when
it no longer shares in their personal struggles. Such a
Church cannot help anyone to love his enemies because
it has forgotten that Christ called men together to be
friends. Yet the problems of war and prejudice, the
touchy questions about belief and belonging together
are solved only by those who can lay down their defenses and open themselves to love. The Church must
help men to deal with what is going on inside them,
with the twisted feelings and failed graces that cut off
love. The Church must be the source of forgiveness and
absolution that frees men from the bondage of the sin
which keeps them apart. This is the most important business for the Church that cares for man.

Beyond this the Church must help men to experience
sureness about the promises God has made. This sureness
is something which permeates all of man. It helps him
to develop a confidence in himself and in his truly human
responses in life. Man needs the security that comes from
the experience of being in touch with the sources of
life, the experience of real sharing with others through
the bond of the Spirit given by God. Man needs this
kind of security but he does not need the security of
overprotection which makes him blind to the real meaning and challenge of life. Security is illusory if it comes
only from preordained plans and formulas of life, with
careful lines drawn here and boundaries set there. The
real security man deserves is the confidence that flows
from a mature understanding of himself and of life
itself. This enables him to face the uncertainties and

unpredictabilities of life with the real resources of his personhood. Life is scored with ambiguity and only the man who is whole can live it truthfully. It is the Church's function to help men face the twisted truths and blind alleys of living with the strength that comes from really understanding the complexities of existence.

The structures of the Church should support and express these functions of service to man. If the structures do not help the Church to carry out these functions effectively, they must be modified or put aside so that the Church can get on with its real business. The institutions cannot take precedence over the persons they are meant to serve. The Church is not a club jealous of its rules and membership. It is rather the home of men. Everything it does must help him to understand and become himself as truly as possible. It is quite clear that institutional reform is demanded when the structures of the Church obstruct rather than facilitate its task of helping man to search, to work, and to love. It is a renewed feeling for the importance of this service which is the impulse of renewal in our day.

Religion, Mature and Immature

Because it has experienced so much of it, the world readily recognizes immature religion. The flaws of half-grown religion have been choice targets for scornful attacks over the centuries. In fact, most charges leveled against religion in general have really been aimed at immature religion in particular. This latter phenomenon, dressed out in magical superstitions and ur-force myths, has never surrendered the fables that were first spoken around the campfires of prehistory. It was Christianity which challenged the primitive views of the universe and freed men from the totems and sun gods which flourished in the imagination of those misty times.

Immature religion has, however, persisted and has managed to give authentic religion a bad name. Incomplete in its view of the universe, fatalistic and wish-fulfilling, it has kept men in bondage to their ancient fantasies and fears. In its name, some men have been manipulated and persecuted, and countless others have been kept at a childish level of religious awareness. The gods of this religion have never been friendly to men. They have been distant and raging forces, showering the world with thunderbolts, boils, and bad luck, and hungering for the worship of appeasement more than the worship of love. They may have laid aside their lightning but they still crouch over the world, inspiring new generations of charms. Compulsions still live in chain letters, magic still makes itself a part of the uneasy faith that rests on unopened letters at Fátima. Immature religion continues to capitalize on fear and on the willingness of men to search for ritualistic patterns and formulas to guarantee salvation.

This is not the religion of the Gospels, not the religion of the inner life of the Spirit which Christ proclaimed. It is the religion of the gods who died, killed by science and higher wisdom, destroyed by man's reflection on its inadequacies. This religion and its trembling deities failed to match the qualities of man's mature personality or to meet his deepest needs. Its residue and regressive magnetism are still discernible in superstition, fanaticism, and in those religious forms which attempt to control rather than free man's potential for growth. One of the meanings of renewal for the Catholic Church is found in its efforts to lay the ghost of immature religious understandings. To this end it searches its own formulations and practices so that they may more adequately express a comprehension of mature religious behavior.

Psychology has pointed out the many differences between mature and immature religion. Undeveloped religion is largely external in its demands and promises. It has been shown that, despite the energy of its practice, it can coexist with ethnic prejudice. This form of religion is not reflective, nor does it demand the change of heart which reorders a person's relationships of faith, hope, and love with other men. It soothes the individual and protects him from the social consequences of a more mature belief. It suffers no crisis because it asks no questions. Mature religion, on the other hand, transforms the inner man, and makes him open to and responsible for others. Full growth in religion emerges from a crisis of questioning and reflection. It is not so shaky that it does not allow a man to doubt and reinspect the religion of his childhood. Mature religion is internalized belief, the convictions of conscience which make a man sensitive to his Christian responsibilities.

According to Gordon Allport, when the religious dimension of personality has come of age it puts away the magical and wish-fulfilling attitudes of childhood. Authentic religion is an all-pervading outlook which takes in the complexities of life realistically and provides a referent of value which enables man to integrate his life experiences. Authentic religion does not offer a simplistic or narrow view. Indeed, it opens man to all of reality, bids him to seek the meaning of it, and contributes to his own full personal growth. Mature religion is hardly the awkward caricature which cynics demolish so zestfully. When religion is fully developed it matches man's needs in a way that no other aspect of his personality does. It broadens his contacts with life, increases his self-awareness, and facilitates the integration of the self.

This kind of religion does not come to a man fullblown. It is subject to the laws of growth and struggle which mark all of man's endeavors. Unfortunately, for one reason or another, men can fail to deal with this aspect of themselves and can cling unthinkingly to immature religious attitudes well into their adult years. It is also true that institutionalized religion prevents true religious growth when it fails to reveal the genuine character and demands of mature religion. Many men hold on to what Allport has called "an essentially juvenile formulation" because they have never been helped to understand anything beyond this. They find childhood religion comforting precisely because it is unquestioning. "They take over the ancestral religion," as Allport says, "much as they take over the family jewels. It would be awkward to bring it into too close a relationship with science, with suffering, and with criticism" (Gordon W. Allport, *The Individual and His Religion,* The Macmillan Co., 1950, p. 52). It is worthwhile to examine the characteristics of mature religion as they have been presented by Allport. It is (1) well differentiated, (2) dynamic in character, (3) productive of a consistent morality, (4) comprehensive, (5) integral, and (6) fundamentally heuristic.

The differentiation of mature religion indicates the broad spectrum of its interests and concerns. It is rich and complex as it takes in every aspect of life. Mature religion is the very opposite of the motivation to accept teachings with uncritical abandon. There is a dynamic of reflection which enables the individual to examine his life experiences and to comprehend the subtle differences and conflicts which sheer emotionalism tends to smooth over. As he grows older, the maturely religious person must examine the religion he received in childhood. Differentiation energizes man's critical faculties but it also demands that he define and put order into his life experience. As a result, mature religion acquaints man with the richness of life and moves him to examine it deeply and without fear. It is not a blind and thoughtless affirmation of a jumble of beliefs and practices. It does not echo the old saw of the pious Catholic as he passes away, "I believe it all, true or false."

The second characteristic of mature religion is its autonomous character and its motivational power. Immature religion, wherever it is found, is mostly concerned with magical thinking, self-justification, and creature comfort. Although the religious outlook derives from many strands of organic and social experience, it is transformed into an independent aspect of personality as the individual matures. It becomes the master rather than the servant of the experiential sources of its development. Mature religion becomes "the best instrument for dealing with life." The person charges it with the "task of interpreting all that comes within its view, and of providing motive power to live in accordance with an adequate frame of value and meaning, and to enlarge and energize this frame" (p. 64). Fully-grown religion is consistently directive as it leads to systematic rather than random moral judgments. Immature religion, on the other hand, generates sporadic and sometimes conflicting moral positions. There is an overall pattern to the fully developed religious outlook. It is not concerned only with "religious" practices, like attending Mass or belonging to a parish. It is not just a social convention. Mature religion applies to all the areas of life.

Immature religion has often made the moral gaze of churchmen seem to be astigmatic and uncertain. They have been selective in their emphasis on the moral questions of life, as is witnessed, for example, by the centuries of preoccupation with sexuality. This is exactly the danger of this immature religious outlook. It keeps man from seeing things in perspective and distorts his sense of values about what is and what is not important in life. Mature religion, on the other hand, presents an integrated view of life in the light of Christian principles and this enables man to make consistent and proportioned moral judgments.

Comprehensiveness is a closely related quality in mature religious behavior. This fits it to the mature mind because it makes sense of all the significant aspects of man's existence. Comprehensive belief makes room for and faces all the facts even when these seem contradictory and very confusing. It provides an outlook which increases tolerance because it is broad and deep in understanding. It not only offers a standard of conduct but it also provides motivation and a sense of satisfaction.

The integral nature of mature religion flows from its comprehensive quality. It brings things together in an intelligible design which fits the period of history and its chief concerns. It is adequate, in other words, to the stage of development in which man finds himself. So, as Allport observes, "the religion we embrace cannot be pre-scientific; nor anti-scientific; it must be co-scientific." Only mature religion makes room for science and provides the principles and energies needed to see that its discoveries are applied to man's life with integrity. Mature religion does not leave out any parts of life merely because it is difficult to fit them into its view of things. Thus mature religion is called to be an ally of science and all other forms of human development. This process of integration is never completed. It is not found in some rigid code but in the flexibility of a religious view which can adapt itself to the process of historical development. There are difficult questions, problems in life such as suffering and evil, which are not easily integrated. Mature religion faces these problems, however, and attempts honestly to work them through. This is one of the most important signs of its maturity.

Finally, authentic religion is heuristic in that it constantly leads man to discover more about himself, the world he lives in, and the teachings of the Gospels. This suggests that mature religion sustains commitment to activity even before all the facts are known with unshakable certainty. As Allport notes, "it can be sure without being cock-sure" (p. 72). This very character of mature religion enables men to take the risks that are necessary for full development. There is not achievement, either personal or social, if men can only move on the grounds of absolute certitude. Mature religion encourages the forward thrust of men to new understandings and new achievements in their relationships and their work. Mature religion urges man out of himself to challenge the forbidding ambiguities of the future with his own sense of purpose. It is generative of hope because it enables men to have faith.

Mature religion contributes to the fulfillment of man by relating him to life in a full-faced and unblinking fashion. It is not fearful or hesitant; it does not influence only marginal areas of human behavior; it is not ordered merely to its own enhancement. Mature religion is not, however, an easy or sentimental option. It is always difficult and challenging. Mature religion always serves man, lighting up the way for him as it challenges him to become more of himself. Genuine religion has a freeing effect on man. It is the very opposite of those immature systems of religious behavior which settle for controlling his growth according to some childish set of pleasingly obedient responses. As such, it is a powerfully sustaining and motivating force. This dramatically transcends the self-interested attitude of childish religion.

Mature religious attitudes are themselves the outcome of growth, growth that is notably affected by the personal relationships of the individual. The home environment and the attitudes of the parents are quite significant in this regard. These are, in turn, shaped very strongly by the attitude of the churches of which they are members. If the Church does not provide a trusting and compassionate view of man and the purpose of his life, then no such vision or attitudes can be handed on to the next generation. It is one of the dangers of institutionalized religion that it can minimize its obligations to personal development because of its concern for structural stability. This, of course, blocks the growth of its members and prevents them from attaining a mature religious outlook.

Mature religion is achieved only if an individual can face and work through the critical moments of his religious development. The most significant of these occurs at the period when he begins to re-examine the religion of his childhood and the complex of instructions and prohibitions which have come to him from others. There comes a time, according to the analysis of Allport, when extrinsic religion must be transformed into intrinsic religion. Extrinsic religion emphasizes an outlook of exclusion. The important thing in extrinsic religion is self-interest, whether it is to achieve praise or to avoid blame and guilt. As an attitude of unquestioning acceptance of what has been given it excludes any experience that may threaten this deposit of belief. Many people who proudly identify themselves with certain religious faiths are actually quite extrinsic in their religious orientation. For them, as Allport has described it (*Religion and Prejudice in Personality and Social Encounter,* Beacon Press, Boston, 1960, p. 264), religion "serves and rationalizes assorted forms of self-interest." Race prejudice is often closely associated with extrinsic religion. Allport's collateral research in this area has demonstrated the common bond between extrinsic religion and prejudice. Both constitute "islands of safety in a threatening world. They are custom tailored life jackets to be donned in frightening waters." Extrinsic religion and prejudice play the same role. They both serve the defensive person through providing a false sense of security which cuts him off from full and open relationships with others.

When a person examines the religion he has received in his childhood he either makes it his own, that is, he internalizes it, or he discards it. If he does not examine it he continues to live according to an extrinsic form of religion. This process usually takes place at a time of crisis which makes him confront his beliefs and his reasons for holding them. This is frequently associated with adolescence, the period of liberation from the family setting. If the person internalizes his beliefs, by working them through in the face of the conflicts or difficulties of his current experience and making them his own, he has taken a step toward mature religion. He no longer operates because someone outside of himself told him this was the right thing for him to do or say or believe. He has hammered out his own conviction so that his subsequent motivation flows from within himself. He passes from the self-centered focus of his earlier religion to a more open and socially-oriented concern. Instead of being afraid of the world or of other men he is ready to be involved in constructive relationship with both. He has achieved what Piaget calls reciprocity, the ability to see that others have convictions and preferences that resemble his own. An isolating point of view is surrendered for one that puts him into a much more mature and constructive position. Intrinsic religion is liberating, as it opens the individual to a life that takes on meaning and direction from internal conviction and a more sensitive understanding of other people. His own interest is no longer the only standard according to which he judges his every action. The individual broadens his vision and operates, as it were, from the inside out. This is the intrinsic religion which Allport found to be free of ethnic prejudice. This is not religion in name only, nor merely a sociological classification by which one defines himself over against others. It is a far deeper and more pervasive aspect of the individual's personality. As such it serves an integrative function insofar as it is the central core around which all the experiences of life can be organized in a genuinely meaningful way. Mature religion provides a theme of life, a reliable foundation that supports a man's work and relationships. It offers a vision which gives him strength and purpose in what can seem a star-crossed world.

The developed religious sense, touching on what is of deepest concern for the person, bids him to put away the things of a child. He is now ready for the real test of living the life of the Spirit. Christianity cannot be understood except as a religion of adults. That it has in many places been relegated, like lifeboats, to women and children illustrates the fact that institutionalized religion has not always responded to the adult needs of mankind. Indeed, Catholicism has suffered from an over-focus on the kind of religious teaching and controls appropriate to the child. It has been exceedingly difficult for many churchmen to put away these childish things. That is why so many people in responsible positions in the Church have always been dismayed by the challenge of the religious cycle of growth. They have chosen to present faith in chunks of teaching that had to be swallowed whole. They possessed the truth and handed it out on the condition that the learners remained passive and gently docile. The teachings had to be accepted on the authority of the teacher who sometimes treated questions as symptoms of infidelity rather than as signs of human struggles. A common seminary rule, until most of these self-destructed in recent years, admonished the students to master their textbooks and to resist asking their professors questions lest they reveal a spirit of contentiousness or pride. The same "take it or leave it" attitude was built into the training of most religious brothers and sisters. These priests and religious in turn became the teachers of religion for the Catholic people. Strange as it may now seem, passivity became the demanded characteristic of generations of believers. The emphasis on doctrine accepted on external authority obviously did not even encourage the individual to look deeply into his belief. Such excursions could only be dangerous to all concerned.

Indeed, the normal process of religious development was powerfully thwarted by this kind of procedure. The individual was not prepared for the moments of questioning which would come as a part of his overall growth to independence. He could not be helped much to internalize his religion when he was conditioned not even to raise questions about it. That fundamentalist line naturally made the person quite dependent on the authority figures of the Church. That gave rise to the brief but soaring lock-step period of Catholic culture in which the good Catholic did what he was told with no questions asked. There may have been a species of Foreign Legion camaraderie among the good soldiers of the Church at that time. There was much emphasis on the romance of following orders, the echoes of which have not all died away. But, like legionnaires, many faithful were wandering in the desert of a childhood belief beyond which they were never allowed to grow.

In recent years theologians and educators have challenged this pedagogy and have worked a revolution in the presentation of the faith. They have been part of the vital movement which was chiefly manifested in the Second Vatican Council. The Church is struggling to put away childish things and to present an adult religious belief to its people. That is part of the dynamic of the turmoil at the present time. These new catechetical approaches, grounded in better theology and psychology, have challenged the authoritarian positions which dominated the teaching of religion for so long. The authoritarian position is indeed under threat but only because there is an effort to preach a more mature religion to Christians. This religion is not afraid of questions or doubts, does not isolate itself in the desert, and emphasizes the profound social responsibilities of the mature Catholic. This new understanding does not suppress inquiry but rather attempts to struggle with men as they deal with their crises of belief. There is an emphasis on the individual's responsibility and a corresponding de-emphasis on forcing him to accept things solely on the word of those outside him. The battle of internal and external religion is going on in the Catholic Church at this very moment.

So closely have many churchmen identified their authority with a reciprocal passivity in the faithful that the present situation is unnerving to them. They have come to believe that any question, legitimate or not, challenges the teaching of the Church. What these questions do, of course, is challenge the Church to be a better teacher, less dependent on control, and more open to the growth problems of its people. The problem the Church has is that of teaching more compassionately and skillfully with a confidence borne of the promises of the Spirit. The problem some churchmen have arises from their failure to resolve the crisis of belief in their own lives. They hold on to a childhood religion and they are afraid to let go. They have not really internalized their faith sufficiently and so the present challenge of renewal is a disturbing personal experience. It seems to them that their authority may be damaged so they respond to present tensions by strenuously reasserting it. This, of course, does more harm to their legitimate authority in the long run than anything else. The teaching authority of the Church obviously suffers if those who possess it do not understand the difference between immature and mature religion.

It is to the credit of a number of American bishops that they have developed a series of annual symposia with scholars from various fields to help them keep up with the advanced developments in theology, Scripture, and, of late, even the social sciences. These bishops are making an effort to deepen their own understanding of the faith and to forward their own process of maturity. They offer a model for the continuing education of other bishops and priests who are charged with proclaiming the truths of the Gospel to all men. This is an important development even though it affects only a small percentage of Church leaders at the present time.

What men need is a Church that is concerned with them as adults. The focus on the child in Catholicism must be changed if mature religious behavior is ever to develop. Indeed, the most important thing that can be done for children is what the Church can do for their parents. The real task lies in responding to their deep need for a religion that is truly the keystone of their total life view. The Church is becoming aware of the inadequacy of keeping a better-educated laity on the level of children in their religious beliefs and practices.

The adult Christian community can put away childish things but only if the Church gives them real food to eat. A more mature faith takes in their home life, their married life, and the whole world of their work and play. It cannot give them pat answers and tell them that if they do not accept them they are being disobedient.

Indeed, some still try this latter approach. Unable to accept the Church as a teacher which must grow in understanding and wisdom, they tell people that if they don't like the Church the way it is, they can get out. But, as Scripture scholar John L. McKenzie has noted, people with a thirst for the truths of faith won't get out. They want to stay in the Church, if only to bother those people who so rigidly insist on their exile. The source of the continued maturity of the Church is in Christians like these who will keep raising questions that remind the Church of its need to grow. The Spirit works through the Christian community, not to pit it against authority, but to place it in closer relationship to it. Churchmen with an immature religious outlook will not survive long when they are surrounded by so many Christians who want to grow up in the Spirit.

It is clear that churchmen must take a long look at what the social sciences have enabled us to understand about the various postures of religious commitment. The authentic followers of Christ must possess a religious belief which is as mature and central to their lives as His was. The Church is supposed to make this a reality for them. It can only do so after it puts away for good the magic and wishes of childhood.

The Church as Counselor
to Conscience

This turbulent age has reminded man of his conscience. Everywhere, in the name of conscience, men take stands that make other men take notice. We have witnessed an increase in conscientious objection to the draft, and the multiplication of radical protests, many of them in the name of reforming the structures of society. The voices of individual conscience, whether they belong to Dr. Spock, draft resisters, or the Berrigan brothers, point out the tension between institutions and interiority. Men always cry out against institutions which seem to diminish rather than enlarge their freedom. The protests of our age are a sign of the overall challenge to institutional forms which substitute regulations for the individual responsibility of conscience.

But individual conscience raises difficult questions. Men speak of "doing their own thing" in our day. This may have a shallow meaning, a slogan for a pseudo-redemption through the liberation of every impulse. It may also point to something more profound, man's determination to be true to himself and his values in life.

The Church has always had the charge of assisting men
in discovering and following their true consciences. Indeed, there is no mature morality unless men are fully
responsible for their own behavior. If the Church is for
men, then it must help them to be adults who are
genuinely responsive to the dictates of conscience.

It is the contention of this chapter that man's conscience develops only when he is helped to develop fully.
The Church must take institutional reform seriously if
it is to carry out its function of forming the Christian
conscience. This is so because the structures of the
Church's relationship to men reflect and express its attitudes about the person. The Church's redemptive mission demands redeeming forms, and this is nowhere more
important than in the question of conscience.

The formation of conscience is a complicated business.
How can a man be sure that he is following his conscience rather than his whims? Is he merely unleashing
his own emotional problems with authority or is he speaking with an anguished but authentic maturity of judgment? Clearly, a perennial task of the Church is the
discernment of spirits. It must help men to understand
and respond to their own fully formed consciences. This
is precisely part of the Church's role as a teacher. When
the Church sets itself properly to the task of aiding men
in the development of their consciences according to
Christian principles, it merits Christ's confident statement
that "he who hears you hears Me."

The formation of Christian conscience is, however, a
subject of intense conflict at the present time. This was
heightened by the discussion which followed *Humanae
Vitae* in which the freedom and the obligations of conscience became a central but very sore point. As a matter
of fact, the teaching of the Church is quite clear. In

the "Decree on Religious Liberty" from Vatican II, the council fathers wrote:

> On his part, man perceives and acknowledges the imperatives of the Divine Law through the mediator of conscience. In all his activity a man is bound to follow his conscience faithfully, in order that he may come to God for whom he was created. (Par. 3)

The Church says that following one's conscience is not a sometime thing. It applies for man "in all his activity." In effect, the council rejects outright any position which says that positive law takes precedence over an individual conscience. The Church, in other words, commits itself to the conscience of man because this is the source of his moral behavior.

The Church cannot carry out this function through churchmen who say to preplexed members of the faithful, "Follow this teaching whether it is right or wrong." This is a scandalous position to take, although it was taken by a Roman cardinal in the fall of 1968. This goes counter to the teaching of Vatican II and to the long tradition of the Church itself. Such a position does serve the ends of the institution, although at the price of sacrificing the interiority of man himself. This outlook is obviously more interested in discipline than truth. This attitude can only be assumed by one who is afraid that the authority of the Church would be seriously imperiled by any reinforcement of the rights of individual conscience. This reveals a long-growing structural weakness in Roman Catholicism which many churchmen had curiously interpreted as a strength. The absolute acquiescence in authoritative decisions which limited or eliminated altogether dissent or further inquiry was a keystone in the monarchical model of the Church. This brought Winston Churchill to observe that only two institutions shared such absolute discipline, Russia and the Roman Church. It is clear that this age has brought a challenge to the disciplinary stances of both of these institutions. A deeper human need and right is being reasserted by men who have become increasingly aware of the precious meaning of individual conscience.

On the other hand, churchmen cannot abandon their responsibility for the formation of conscience by merely stepping back and leaving men on their own. Unfortunately, many churchmen far beneath the ranks of the hierarchy have adopted this mode of reaction. For them freedom of conscience becomes an escape hatch from their role in man's struggle for a mature moral outlook. Because the situation about birth control, for example, became so confusing, many priests have said, in effect, to their congregations: "Follow your own conscience," without providing either the teaching or the understanding their people need in order to do this. This may make these churchmen feel less anxious, but it is, in the argot of the age, a copping out on one of their most serious responsibilities. They need not have all the answers, but they are never excused from sharing in man's search, in the light of Christian principles, for the right answers.

Psychological research has provided evidence that man's moral development takes place in stages. It matches, in other words, his overall process of personal development. Following this initial suggestion by Jean Piaget, Lawrence Kohlberg was able to distinguish six types of morality ranging across three levels of development. He was also able to provide illustrations of behavior for these different stages. These have been schematized by Ernest Hilgard in the following manner:

Stage	*Illustrative Behavior*
Level I. *Premoral*	
Stage 1. Punishment and obedience orientation.	Obeys rules in order to avoid punishment.
Stage 2. Naive instrumental hedonism.	Conforms to obtain rewards, to have favors returned.
Level II. *Morality of conventional role-conformity.*	
Stage 3. "Good-boy" morality of maintaining good relations, approval of others.	Conforms to avoid disapproval, dislike by others.
Stage 4. Authority maintaining morality.	Conforms to avoid censure by legitimate authorities with resultant guilt.
Level III. *Morality of self-accepted moral principles*	
Stage 5. Morality of contract, of individual rights, and of democratically accepted law.	Conforms to maintain the respect of the impartial spectator judging in terms of community welfare.
Stage 6. Morality of individual principles of conscience.	Conforms to avoid self-condemnation.

Where would most Catholics find themselves in this diagram? In the mind-set that aims at preserving the authority and the discipline of the institution, few would be permitted to go beyond the level of conventional role-conformity. This is exactly the experience of many Catholics who have been made so dependent on voices outside of themselves for approval that they have never been able to hear the voice of their own conscience. This is the level of development which was allowed when there was an emphasis on the manipulation of guilt in the pastoral practice of the Church. This was, of course, an immature corruption of the pastoral relationship of the Gospels. It is striking, for example, to note what great freedom Christ gave even to his closest friends. He did not compel people to follow him nor did he manipulate them in small but telling ways. He proclaimed the truth and always held himself open in relationship to others. He did not, however, use force. That was something the Church took to itself at a later date. It is the guilt machine, as I have noted earlier, which was broken down in our day. It does not work very well any more. This merely signifies that the Church has a new opportunity to re-establish itself in its relationship as moral teacher to mankind.

The Kohlberg study implies that the overall growth of the human being is vitally important to the achievement of an inner-directed morality. Religion cannot be made intrinsic except by men who are fully grown in all aspects of their personality. Each stage of moral development, then, builds on a previous stage. It is the function of the Church to contribute to the thorough development of its individual members so that they may attain the freedom of the sons of God. To insist on overcontrol on the one hand or to abandon relationship altogether on the other, is to fail mankind in an issue of fundamental importance. Both these positions represent defensive postures as well as a clear repudiation of the constant teaching of the Church about the vital role of individual conscience. Men who lack inner freedom cannot respond to the Spirit. Freedom of conscience is not an option but a necessary quality for Christian living.

When the Church takes its function of helping men to form their consciences seriously, it is acting in its role as teacher. It does not, however, merely utter principles from afar. The principles of the Christian life are to be taught as they are found in the Gospels. This message cannot, however, be addressed merely to the intellectual side of man. This is not the way the person operates. Knowledge is not virtue, and intellectual information, in itself, is not enough to help man to the good life. Indeed, man has been perennially puzzled by the fact that he often knows the right thing to do and yet, somehow or other, it can still be very difficult to do it. The person operates as a unity, not by parts of himself. He cannot develop morally unless the whole of his personality, intellect and emotions, mind and body, grow together in an integrated manner.

Conscience is not some separate entity which comes full-blown or which grows on its own. It is the expression of the person, of his overall orientation toward himself and toward others in the framework of his state in life. Conscience manifests the manner in which he has integrated his values and experiences so that he understands who he is at each point of moral choice. Conscience is the sounding of the true self with all the interlocking aspects of feeling and reason which go into the making of a man. It is, as Allport says, the "fine edge" of personality. Conscience, as Donald L. Berry has put it ("The

Rhetoric of Conscience," *The Christian Century*, September 4, 1968), is:

> the voice of this intricate fabric of trust and loyalties, not some private voice discontinuous with the rest of our life; when conscience guides us, we are guiding ourselves from the depths of decisions and loves that have made us what we are.

Conscience is not a blind and autonomous faculty. It is rather the product of fully human development which enables a person to look into himself and to take responsibility for his actions because he understands their source and their meaning in the light of Christian principles. It is clear that an important part of what humanizes man is his religious faith. A man's religious faith opens him to the Spirit of Truth which illumines the complexities of life with the light of the Gospels. The process of his personal growth will cause an individual to confront the nature of his religious belief and to yield up those aspects which were appropriate only in his childhood. He cannot be religiously mature unless he has internalized his belief. It is in this most sensitive area of growth where the Church must stand at man's side as a knowledgeable and understanding teacher. The Church cannot help men to mature if it stands at the head of the class, birching rod at the ready, fearful that the questions or difficulties of its students will somehow destroy its authority. This is a poor method for any teacher. A good teacher hears his students, tries to sense their problems and to respond to them so that they can freely learn. His gift to them is not just information, but the discovery of themselves which enables them to enter into life. This is much more what the stance of the Church as teacher must be if it is to interact effectively with growing man.

The Church must reactivate its traditional role of "wise counselor" to man. The Church through its servants must be ready to explore with man the host of personal difficulties which impede his growth and which make the development of a true conscience difficult. A teacher never sacrifices his authority when he is able to move sensitively with human beings who would learn from him. In fact, unless he is able to do this, people will probably not learn much from him at all. A real teacher demonstrates his sureness when he is able to join his resources of wisdom and vision to the struggles of those for whom he has responsibility.

The Church proclaims the Gospel but it also struggles with men as they try to incorporate these teachings in their lives. It is for the Church to create an atmosphere in which moral development will take place because overall personal development takes place. A fear of growth, the inability to trust, and the insistence on classroom-like discipline all go against creating this environment of growth. Man does look into himself when he has the atmosphere that really frees him to do so. Perhaps the Church needs to refurbish its contemplative heritage, not just for monks with a special calling, but so that the world may have a quiet and unpressured place in which to examine its conscience. It may, in other words, be a form of service to mankind which is desperately needed during a turbulent age.

To speak of the Church as a counselor to the conscience of mankind is not to strip it of its supernatural role for the sake of a contemporary analogy. All that modern counselors and psychotherapists have really done is to rediscover the understanding of man that is found in the Gospels. Man is unitary, trustworthy, and capable of facing the truth about himself when we give him a chance to do it. The Church took on other more authoritarian postures toward men for a variety of reasons during the course of history. At a time of renewal the Church must reclaim its Gospel attitudes toward persons. Failing to do this, the Church only compounds its own problem of failing to see man whole. It further removes itself from the possibility of redemptive dialogue with man.

A counselor must have certain uncluttered ideas about himself before he can begin to help others. If he presumes that he knows everything, he tends to impose solutions on those who come to him. This is particularly true if he has a need to impress the other, to bolster his own authority, or to protect himself from healthy involvement with his patient. These defenses must be dropped before the therapist can really present himself as a helper to anyone. To accomplish this, he looks into himself and examines his own conscience as it reveals the thrust of his personality in relationship to others. This is a quite ordinary procedure for the therapist because he realizes that he must know the truth about himself before he can join himself to his patient's search for truth.

The therapist also learns to listen so that he can truly hear what his patient is saying or struggling to put into words about his own internal experience. The counselor fails if he presumes to understand the problem before the other has even expressed it. The counselor is of little help if he cuts off the other, offers too much advice from his own viewpoint, or spends the time talking about his own problems. It is as the counselor joins in the toil of therapy, the shared and at times painful journey into the depths of the patient, that growth begins. The patient begins to accept and identify his true personality and to sort out the complex strands of his motivation. He discovers the truth about himself and begins to take control over his own behavior in a more mature way. The patient, in other words, becomes more responsible for himself as the judgments of his conscience come into sharper focus.

The therapist also knows how to confront or to face his patient with the truth about reality. This is a delicate process which requires both wisdom and sensitivity. It is not accomplished through the blundering kind of attack which destroys and discourages the patient. Confrontation requires the counselor to love the other enough to point out his defenses or evasions. His is the voice of the real world which prevents the patient from escaping his obligations to life by constructing a world of his own. The counselor then remains in relationship with the struggling person, sharing even the burden of his reaction to the confrontation. All this is done to free the patient to face the truth about himself as responsibly as possible.

No therapist does these things, of course, unless he believes that his patient is capable of taking charge of his own life. His commitment to the struggling person evidences a genuine respect for and trust in the individual's own strength. The therapist's personal commitment is to the promise of growth that marks the nature of man. These attitudes, among others, are basic for parents, teachers, or anyone else who would aid others in attaining their maturity. The development of a reliable moral conscience is linked essentially to the total process of personal growth. This is markedly affected by the amount of trust and respect a person experiences in his most important life relationships.

The Church must look on man in a similar fashion if it is to help him reach the judgments about himself and his own behavior that flow from a mature conscience. The Church, first of all, must believe in man and place itself at his side as he looks into the depths of his personality. There will be little real help if the Church chooses not to trust man's God-given potential for growth.

So too, the Church must understand its own motivations in its efforts to form a Christian conscience. Does it present itself as a loving and freeing friend of man who asks nothing except that man achieve fullness of responsibility? Or does it try to impose solutions for man which short-circuit the growth process? Does it manipulate man into an uncomfortable obedience to authority or does it give him the freedom to find and act in accord with his real self? Is the Church interested in the individual person or in bolstering its own structures? Does it listen to man or insist that man must be the listener in his relationship to the Church? Does the Church open itself to the problems of man, even those he has difficulty in expressing, or does it merely lose itself in its own problems? When the Church confronts the conscience of others with Gospel principles, does it do so with a continuing and compassionate presence? A Church which truly understands its vocation of service must obviously be a sensitive counselor to wayfaring man or it will contribute little to the growth of well-informed and responsible conscience.

The Church does not form the conscience of men in isolation from one another. The social dimension of Christianity offers one of the basic points of reference for the person. He finds his true conscience in relationship to the Christian community, to the Church as a people. This indeed presents a test of reality for his own personal decisions. Do they match the convictions of the Church as a community of service to the world? Do his decisions make him a more responsible neighbor to all those who are in need? The well-formed Christian conscience is personal but it is never completely private. This is so because the person only grows in relationship to others. The resolution of his conscience does not leave him a solitary figure in the cosmos. It makes him more aware of his relationship to others and his responsibilities in regard to the growth of the community in which he lives. His commitment to Christian principles, to the discovery of God's will for him, always demands a fuller and more vital relationship to his fellow men. The Church, with great sensitivity and understanding, always confronts the individual as a member of Christ's servant community.

It is clear that the Church cannot remind men of their communitarian obligations in conscience unless it strives constantly to purify its presence as a community of faith and love in the world. In other words, the structures of the Church must express the nature of the People of God as a mystery of human relationships or the Church will have difficulty in developing mature consciences in its members. It cannot sensitize men to the social referent of conscience if it presents itself in the form of an authoritarian organization. This only heightens the conflict about freedom of conscience because it contrasts institutional demands with the interiority of the individual Christian life.

Institutional reform is, then, intimately related to the effective proclamation of the traditional teaching that

men must, in all their activity, follow the judgment of
their conscience. If the institutional overlay of Christianity cripples the Church's ability to interact with persons as members of a real community, then the institutions must be reformed so that this can once again take
place. The present tension about questions of conscience
is related to the fact that many accidental structures
of the Church are too authoritarian in nature to permit
the Church to carry out its function of serving as the
wise counselor in the moral development of individuals.
Some churchmen are too intent on preserving these dys-
functional forms to understand the need to revise them
for the sake of the people who are the Church. These
churchmen generate conflict because they do not listen
to the voices of Christian experience. Although they are
sure that they have the answers, in reality they do not
even hear the questions. They put their energies into institutional preservation rather than into the institutional
transformation that would free the Church to serve man
more effectively. This tactic, in the name of preserving
Church structures, only leads to greater drift away from
the Church on the part of men who seek to lead their
lives with a Christian conscience. It leads to men doing
their own thing uninformed by the Gospels or by the
experience of the Christian community. The Church is
then in danger of losing its pastoral relationship altogether. This does happen when churchmen lose sight of
their commitment to the growth of their people. They
lose also their real authority as teachers and counselors
to mankind because they have concentrated on preserving a spurious authoritarianism under the guise of maintaining a deceptive institutional stability.

Men need the Church and the truth about the resurrected life which it is called to share with them. They

stumble blindly and confusedly when the light of the Gospels is denied to them. The Church which has clearly defined itself as man's servant must renew its relationship to men through a healthy reformation of its institutional presence. The emphasis must be on opening itself to growing man rather than on holding on to the authoritarian positions which have put it at a distance from him. It is only in the context of a renewed relationship to the person that the Church can speak with the authority of wholehearted service to him.

Sexuality—
Who Has the Problem?

It is no secret that man has been uneasy about his sexuality for centuries. The present pan-erotic state of culture is the explosive overreaction to and evidence of the ineffective repressive defenses that operated for such a long period. Man has a new understanding of himself and of the paramount value of his whole personality in relationship to others. The dynamism of this rediscovery of the self has shattered the taboos and the embarrassed silence of history about man's sexuality.

Many aspects of the Church have not made history; they have instead been made by history. Consequently, the fresh view of man and the institutions such as marriage which were meant to celebrate his fullness, have been clouded in the process. Gradually, and at times unconsciously, the Church absorbed the anxieties of its environment. This is particularly true about sexuality. Just as gradually it has institutionalized viewpoints about man which have contradicted or confused its own understanding of the human person.

This process of the institutionalization of incomplete understandings about man has been subtle. It is only now, as it searches itself for its lost vision of redeemed man, that the Church has come to confront the defenses it acquired over the years. These defenses have manifested themselves in many of the laws and regulations of its pastoral practice regarding marriage, celibacy, and the forms of life which it has designed for priests and religious. Less obvious but underlying all of these has been the institutionalization of attitudes toward sexuality which have made the Church hesitant to contemplate clearly or to deal straightforwardly with sexuality. These attitudes, with their roots in emotion rather than reason, are far more resistant to reform than intellectual pronouncements. Indeed, in external words, the Church has reiterated, from Chalcedon to Vatican II, its commitment to authentically incarnational values. These statements, however, have not been completely effective in maintaining an open and understanding view of man in practice. Churchmen have never fully purged themselves of the emotional blocks about sexuality which they developed in the course of history. These, however, remain as the defenses which must be put aside if the Church is to achieve its identity in the modern world.

The selective attention which has been given, for example, to the teachings of St. Augustine on marriage has contributed to the ecclesiastical prejudice against sexuality as a healthy element of life. Certain texts of Augustine tended to disparage sex, despite his overall praise of marriage. Sexual desire in and for itself was regarded, even in marriage, as a result of sin and as "evil" concupiscence. Marriage, as an institution, was considered a *remedium concupiscentiae*, a "cure for concupiscence." The overtones of uneasiness about sex as barely tolerable made marriage a tenuously acceptable outlet in the emotional life of the Church. This emotional coloring gave rise to the notion that marital intercourse defiled a person in some way. The use of marriage made a person unworthy to receive the Eucharist. Gradually religion and human love were dissociated in the attitude of Church teachers. As Nietzsche said, Christians for centuries begot children with a bad conscience.

This subsurface anxiety, this general attitude about the evils of sexuality, was symbolized in a variety of all-too-familiar practices. This included the disproportionate exaltation of virginity under the guise of a supposedly higher and more supernatural morality. Marriage, as Franz Arnold has noted (*Woman and Man,* Herder and Herder, New York, 1963, p. 119), was thought of as a "'slow train' to heaven as compared with the 'express' represented by the evangelical counsels." This emotional block also institutionalized itself in the tendency of some moralists to regard sexual intercourse under the heading of venial sin. It showed itself in incidental institutionalizations such as the calendar of saints where very few husbands and wives found a place, although it was thronged with saintly monks and virgins. In the same way this prejudice against sex lay beneath the emphasis on women who were only able to consecrate themselves wholly to the Lord after their husbands had either died or voluntarily, if reluctantly, retired to monasteries.

In the same way the Church overemphasized the procreation of children as the sole primary end of marriage. This has been redressed by Vatican II, but the emotional residue of this distorted emphasis still remains. It may have been this underscoring of children as the center of marriage that reinforced certain attitudes which oriented religion to the level of the child as well. In failing to emphasize the relationship of husband and wife, the Church has been child-oriented for a long time. Not allowing itself to comprehend the vitality of the parents' relationship as the source of the health and growth of the children, the Church has quite unconsciously neglected its commitment to adults. It is just possible that, because of this, the Church has neglected to develop fully the qualities of mature religious behavior. It has not dealt fully with mature sexuality and so it has not dealt fully with man.

All this suggests that certain churchmen have been suffering from a problem concerning sex. This is not to identify their attitudes with the traditional teaching of the Church, which, once one has removed the overgrowth of history, is clearly a joyous celebration of man and his sexuality. Indeed the Scriptures still astound the prudish with their openness to man as a sexual being. It was no accident that Paul described Christ's relationship to the Church as that of husband and wife. The defenses that have made some churchmen uneasy about the healthy exuberance of the Gospels about man have been the signs of the problem. It has been a self-perpetuating problem, particularly because of the strongly institutionalized preparation of priests and religious, but it is one that must be faced and dealt with if the Church is to recover its role of servant to man. But the problem is not out there. It is in the emotional life of the Church, that is to say, in the emotional lives of churchmen.

Churchmen with this problem are, however, only being true to their training. They were formed in institutions which flowered from the defensive ground of previous generations. These institutions are hardly to be identified with Christ's Church. They developed as the concrete embodiments of the mind-set which slowly developed out of distortions in the Christian view of the person. These institutions hardened in the Counter Reformation era and with them hardened an aloof and mistrustful outlook on sexuality. That they produced men and women with these same attitudes is not surprising. Much of the Church's present ferment arises precisely because this institutionalized training is no longer effective for those who would serve the Church.

The pre-eminent sign of this institutionalized view of life is the awkward way in which Church leaders still respond to the sexual problems of man. Few subjects stir so much supposedly righteous indignation from the pulpits of Christendom. One is reminded of these Church leaders by the comments of sociologist William Simon concerning the sexual revolution in the United States:

> The so-called sexual revolution has little to do with the preoccupations of the young but a lot to do with the preoccupations of the old, particularly their anxieties and fantasies about the young people enjoying something they have missed.
>
> New York *Times*, November 15, 1968

All the perfervid pronouncements about sex betray the defensiveness of leaders who still view morality as primarily sexual morality. They have not cleared their heads of the Platonic notion that the body is the tomb rather than an organ of the soul. Interestingly enough, the people on the receiving end of the admonitions about sex seem quite able, with a little encouragement and understanding, to place sex in a much healthier perspective.

It is frequently embarrassing to hear some churchmen

speak about love. As a matter of fact, you seldom hear them speak about the subject. They usually prefer to speak of "charity." More often than not this is the institutionalized brand related to the annual Catholic Charities collection. Berdyaev (*The Destiny of Man*, London, 1937) once complained of the Christian preachers who denied the significance of love and who seemed to condemn love itself. Sex, love, and marriage, he wrote, "are associated with procreation but not with personality or with the lives of individuals."

It seems strange that the spokesmen for the Church, whose members were to be recognized because they loved one another, are so ill at ease with this topic. This is because they are ill at ease with the basis of life itself, human relationships, and so words about man, love, and sexuality come haltingly, if at all, from their lips. One is, at times, reminded of D. H. Lawrence's description of "the gray disease of sex hatred, coupled with the yellow disease of dirt lust." In any case, sex has seldom been spoken of in an unself-conscious way. It has more often than not been spoken of in terms of something that is questionable and clouded at best. Uneasy churchmen can make the word *pure* sound dirty when they speak it in isolation from an understanding of the human person.

It is not, as has been mentioned, the fault of churchmen that they have gotten out of touch with man. They have labored, because of their training, under the burden of outworn and unuseful perceptions. The model of man which was presented to them in the seminary, both for the understanding of themselves and for their work with others, was hardly the Christian view of unitary man. It was a corrupted and degraded view, man the beast. No wonder they have felt that their duty in life was to build cages for men. Too many churchmen have lost all touch with the physical, since they have been influenced by the attitude that this is evil or less than worthy of man's spirit. They have consequently lost any sense of the healthy earthiness of man. Sexuality has been intellectualized so long that it has become an entity which is not at all integrated in the overall attitude of many churchmen toward life. They may think they know all about it and they may speak that way. They are speaking, however, about something that is largely the product of their own imagination and which is seldom related to the experience of the Christian community.

It is no news to the world that many churchmen cannot understand, much less accept, sexuality as eminently human. They really blush when the notion of the erotic is brought up, and yet this is also human and healthy when it is understood properly. Feelings of sexuality, unless we are to betray the Incarnation, were experienced by Christ Himself. They are not unknown to any man who is capable of sensing and giving the right name to his own experience in life.

The heritage of a faulty understanding of man has been quite pervasive in the Catholic tradition of the last few centuries. This has caused an enormous amount of suffering, especially because of those churchmen who have projected their own problem out on the faithful. This distorted view of man is in itself a repudiation of the way man is perceived in the Gospels. Unitary man has been divided, according to this view, into spirit and flesh, intellect and emotions. If one has this mistaken notion of man in mind it is very difficult to relate to him as he really is. That explains why the Church has done so little at times to help men reach the depths of their own being, why it has failed to help them sense and discover their own rich potential. It has been easier to stand outside of man, to condemn and to control him rather than to understand and encourage him. Church-men have found it easier to warn of the dangers of the journey of life than to struggle with man the wayfarer.

It is probably because of this unsatisfactory view of man that the statistical concept of Christianity has come to full flower. It is, after all, much easier to treat man as a number than as a human person. So we have been concerned over the years with the number of baptisms, the size of the parish, the wealth of the diocese, or, in what continues to be a source of puzzlement if not scan-dal to the world, the riches of the Vatican, with its intricate and extensive investments and with the stran-gling burden of the accumulated trinkets of the centuries. One might wonder, in passing, just how much displaced sexuality has motivated the acquisition of wealth and power on the part of churchmen at different times dur-ing history. We have put into museums the terrible herit-age of misunderstanding man.

Sex has also been a primary area for manipulating the guilt feelings of others. If men avoided "dirty" thoughts, if they held themselves properly aloof from all occasions of sin, they were freed from the anxiety that they would experience from the thought that they might have sinned. Since sexuality is such an all-pervading part of human personality, the skillful ecclesiastical manipulator could really catch man coming and going in almost any area of life where he experienced sexual feelings. It is difficult to understand why churchmen took to themselves such authority over the internal emotional life of others. There is, nonetheless, no denying that sex was *the* sin and that a measure of Christian virtue was our ability to avoid even acknowledging the experience of our own sexuality.

That led one college girl, who had been subjected to the scouring effect of sixteen years of Catholic school non-sex education, to explain, with a wisdom all her own, "I am so pure I float."

The Church has betrayed, in its attitude toward human sexuality, an overall failure to appreciate with complete sensitivity the human condition. This faltering feeling for man has led churchmen to distort and misemphasize the Gospel teachings over the centuries. The balance is only now being redressed, although many churchmen continue to fight a desperate rear-guard action. This, however, clearly reveals their own problem in this matter. The younger generation is far more relaxed than the older in facing the meaning of sexuality in life. Howsoever the mistaken notions of sex insinuated themselves into the attitude of the Church, they were magnificently preserved by the style of training to which most priests, sisters, and brothers were exposed. According to a most extraordinary insight the best way to prepare them to serve the world was to move them out of it into a highly artificial and stylized environment and then to reinsert them into the world in an equally artificial and stylized environment. As classic examples of total institutions, seminaries and religious houses were able to control the entire environment of the candidates who entered them. The environment of the religious house was coextensive with the environment of the young men and women who were there for training. They were not allowed out and their contact with their families and with the news of current events were severely limited if not eliminated altogether.

This was a very strange process. It is my theory that most of the training in seminaries and houses of studies did very little to form the character of the priests and religious who managed to survive them. What it did, to some extent, was to provide a test for healthy personalities who, it has been shown in a great variety of other unfortunate circumstances, can endure a great deal and still not lose the fundamental normality which they derived from their parents and families in the first place. Unfortunately, however, one of the prime objectives of the training period was to distract a person from his sexuality and to condition him to avoid sexual feelings and all those experiences which might give rise to them. In other words, training houses, instead of producing more fully-grown men and women, tended to neutralize their personalities, to make of them a third thing. When an institution can control completely the environment of its subjects, it can go a long way in achieving this kind of conditioning effect.

The result of this, for many priests and religious, was to arrest their growth in adolescence. Their growth was stopped because of the repressive attitudes which kept them in a preadolescent stage of psychosexual development. It is a terrible indictment of those minds which originally contrived these systems of training to see the effects this had on those who were subjected to this experience.

One of the tasks of the adolescent is to integrate his sexual feelings into his personality. This does not mean that it is a time of license or any and all kinds of sexual adventure. It means, quite simply, that a person has to become acquainted with and understand his own inner experience and sense it as an important part of his developing self. Formation programs emphasized many collateral values, such as docility and unquestioning obedience, which also prevented the individual from completing the adolescent task of learning how to relate to authority.

It is not surprising to find that subjects remained at a preadolescent level of development. This is not to say that those who ran these houses of formation understood what they were doing, nor that they really wanted to do this. What they wanted was to keep their subjects obedient, willing, and preserved from any dangers of violating celibacy or chastity. They paid an enormous price, or rather their subjects did, for this entirely unhealthy means of preparing them for life. It was, however, functional insofar as their subjects were under the control of a tightly supervised environment. That was why it was necessary to extend this environment, in terms of the life styles of rectories and convents, after the person was ordained or professed.

This also explains why, after ordination or profession, so much of what had been repressed about sexuality came to the fore in the lives of priests and religious. This could also, I suspect, be applied to the graduates of highly restrictive Catholic colleges. Sex will out, especially when the individual begins to have life experiences which are different from the very closely controlled ambiance of his previous training. For example, there was the displacement of sexuality into many other activities in the lives of priests and religious. This can obviously be seen in those whose whole lives have been devoted to the acquisition of power or to the control of the lives of other people. It can likewise be seen in those who give considerably energy over to the acquisition of wealth, the development of coteries, or the comforts of life.

Many developed an excessive concern for health, a hypochondriacal adjustment which centered very much on the self. I remember a priest talking about a colleague and saying, "His medicine chest is so full we should call him Father Parke-Davis." A great deal of psychosomatic complaint attended this kind of adjustment. The real cause, mishandled or unhandled sexuality, was seldom even suspected. And, of course, no one was even to speculate about such hidden motivations. One might quickly be dismissed as a faithless "Freudian."

More obviously, there were crises of alcoholism and homosexuality in the lives of those who had never come to terms with their own personalities. Sadly, there has been more of this than anybody would like to admit. Few have really tried to look deeply into the roots of these problems. In fact, problems like psychosomatic illness, alcoholism, and homosexuality were relatively easy to handle once the person had acted out this problem sufficiently. Once, in other words, he or she had cried loudly enough for help through overt behavior, they were sent to the doctor or were institutionalized. It was their fault and frequently they were treated as though they were receiving a punishment instead of a therapeutic experience.

It is a strange but true fact that many superiors can tolerate and deal with unhealthy problems better than they can deal with healthy people whose adjustment is quite normal. That is to say, the one thing many superiors cannot stand is the priest or religious who mystifies them by being able to love other people and who is, therefore, loved in return. This natural and quite reasonable course of events seems a contradiction to the cold process of neutering that became the ideal in preparation for the priesthood and religious life. It is a scandal that the hyperactive imagination of many superiors leads them to mistrust and misjudge their healthiest members when they develop wholesome relationships with each other or with their people. They can, for example, tolerate a sister who develops a neurotic illness and never does another lick of work for the rest of her life. They do not, however, know what to do with a woman religious who is able to deal effectively and lovingly with those she teaches or with whom she works. She is a puzzle and a challenge to the repressive processes which are the symptoms of a very sick system.

It is not surprising, in the light of all of this, to find that the clerical attitude has been defensive in dealing with human sexuality. It merely shows how effective the conditioning of their training years really was. It explains the resurgence of adolescent problems in so many priests and religious whose growth was suspended for a number of years while the old tight and controlled world of Catholicism was still functioning smoothly. Nor is it surprising that they would transfer their uneasy attitudes to the faithful. In fact, many developed a morbid curiosity about the sexual lives of their people, using reaction-formation as a defense against admitting their own problems to themselves. They could measure, count, and categorize sexual feelings, always putting them under the heading of grave matter, always ready to label them as a mortal sin. It is not strange that an unhealthy psychology developed which said that the very "first movements" of sexual reactivity were sinful. This constituted an immediate indictment of the utterly human. It also explains the generally negative and unhealthful outlook that has been so hurting to sincere Christians everywhere.

It explains as well the awkward way in which celibacy and birth control are discussed in the contemporary Church. These discussions are self-conscious and never entirely free from the overtones of people who are not sure whether sexuality is something healthy or not. In the echoes of distorted Augustinian teaching, sex is, at best, a concession. To admit otherwise would rob churchmen of the defenses they have so elaborately established against this area of human experience. The saddest part of all this is the amount of suffering that has been caused to so many people because of the failure to treat sexuality in a straightforward and honest manner. It explains the bitter fruit of maladjustment in the lives of so many priests and religious who were so poorly trained to minister to the human needs of men. It is this entire structure of defense which is crumbling because of the insights into man as a human person which have been developed so deeply in this very century.

The institutionalization of unhealthy attitudes toward sexuality has made it difficult for even the healthiest servants of the Church to place themselves in relationship to the Christian community. In the name of keeping priests and religious safe from the world, outmoded institutions have emphasized a neutrality of relationship which has robbed many of their vigor as men and women. That is why there have been so many cries of pain on the part of priests and religious who have sensed that, in the suffocating institutionalization of their lives, they have never come to terms with their own manhood or womanhood. This also explains the depth of feeling that is so widespread against the institutional Church. They are angry at the institutional forms that developed over the centuries because these left little room for their growth as individuals.

This heavy overinstitutionalization of the training and living conditions of priests and religious robbed many of them of any creativity in their life and work. That is always the toll exacted from men and women who are not helped to deal positively with their own sexuality. They were conditioned to a system that served institutional rather than human ends. It is small wonder that so much bitterness is now being experienced toward the institutions which brought atrophy instead of life to so many. This psychological impotence, this inability to respond promptly and creatively to the challenge of renewing Church structures, is itself a sign of just how badly the institutions of the Church need renewal at this time.

It is clear that the Church has a problem with sexuality which cannot be responded to by rejecting renewal or by the authoritarian reinforcement of moribund structures. It is a deep problem which has affected the creative resources of its personnel in a profound way. The institutions which gave rise to and which continue to cause this problem must be refashioned if the Church is to place itself once again in the relationship of servant to all men. Hope arises from the fact that institutionalized prejudices against sexuality are being exposed in our day as the crippling defenses they truly are. Christ's Church lies beneath these defenses and the Spirit is strengthening it to put them aside. The Church is at last dealing with sexuality and, although the struggle is painful and confusing, it can only lead to fullness of relationship to mankind.

The Things That Last

Doctrine is not a way of life any more than teaching theology is the same as proclaiming the Gospel. If we ask what it means to have faith, we do not look for a compendium of statements. We are concerned rather with a way of life and the foundation values that give it both direction and sustenance. Belief, for the ordinary man, refers to the things he bets his life on. The theological content of his belief finds a test and an expression in the experience of his life, in the nature and qualities of his relationships with other people.

Christ invited men into relationship with Him. "I have called you friends," He said in a clear emphasis on the fact that the Christian life reveals itself in the way we walk with one another. "Believe in Me," He said, strongly emphasizing the personal nature of Christian faith. In the same way, He did not say "Follow these directions," but "Follow Me." Over and over He emphasized the fact that those who drink from the wells of living water do not merely commit themselves to a set of theological propositions. They commit themselves to living in the way Christ did. His kind of language cuts right to the heart of the matter for Christians. In very human terms Christ tells us that faith is reflected in a way of life much more than in a way of thinking about life.

This same direct language characterized the Gospels when they were first written. It describes in homely terms how men get on with each other when they are truly united in the Spirit. The Gospel language is refreshing because it gets us back to reality. A strange religious language developed over the centuries, a lace-edged ecclesiasticalese noted for its booming rhetoric. This is the language that has made faith something of a mystery, the language that has relegated religious behavior to a corner of life which is illumined by a single shaft of stained-glass light. Most people do not really like religious language although they labor under the notion that they are supposed to. In their hearts they long for words that speak to their experience as human beings, words that give life and courage. This is the kind of language that Christ spoke. It is to human experience that we must turn if we are to understand anything about real faith.

Faith, like the original writing of the Gospels, was made for men, most of whom are quite ordinary and unsophisticated as they try to make their way through the antagonistic currents of life. Faith is essential for men. Without it they cannot stay alive at all. Faith is something which the Church should be good at. It refers, in the order of human experience, to the way a man opens himself up to other people and to the world around him. Faith makes sense out of moving into the darkness before one has plotted all the moves of a journey. It is faith that opens men to friendship and love. Through it they can count on each other and hope for the best in each other. It is the underpinning of love, both for falling into it and staying in it with another person. Faith is what a man runs out of when he is up against things and his friends seem to have deserted him. Faith plants the seeds of the future, hope nourishes them, and love brings them to full growth. These are three things at the very heart of life, three things that last.

Faith is an unusual compound of the kinds of experience only humans have. Risk and trust are always present, the one inextricably bound up with the other, part of the same pulse beat in the heart of man. Time, man's relentless companion, adds another dimension because faith is found now, at the present moment, but it links man with his past and opens him to his future. Value is there, transcending logic as man searches for the things he will live by. Faith is filled with struggle, the effort of life that is the opposite of neurotic restlessness. Faith is anything but blind as it confronts the demand of life's struggle. It understands the odds and challenges them constantly. So too, authentic faith is not the immature flight into magic, the escape hatch that leads to a story-book world. Indeed, faith turns a man full-faced toward reality, holding his focus almost painfully on the tasks for which he is responsible. Faith does not inhabit a world of shadows and wishes. It has more to do with moving the mountains of everyday obligations than it does with miracles. Faith is vital as the strength of man undefended against the hard edges of real life.

Man becomes aware of his faith when he has to draw upon it. It may be the product of what the most important people in his life have done for him but he cannot face his own problems with their faith. There is no doubt that the manner of relationship of his parents, teachers, and priests is more important in the development of his faith than any particular thing they ever said to him. If they were trusting and respectful of his person, if they were loving and open to letting him discover his true self, if they were, in other words, real Christians, then they helped build his faith. They gave him some of the strength which they lived by, a strength he feels when the contradictory winds of life blow across his own world. Faith prepares a man for crises; it does not inoculate him against them. Man faces a primary crisis of faith in the challenge to internalize the beliefs which he has received from others during his formative years. The Chinese have a two-part symbol for crisis. Half of it means "danger," but the other half means "opportunity." So it is with this crisis, a normal one in the maturation of religion. So it is with all the subsequent crises of life. The Greek origin for *crisis* means decision. This is precisely what a man must make at some point in the course of his development, a decision about the meaning of life, God, moral obligations, and the use of his own freedom. It is the kind of choice a man should be prepared for but from which he cannot be protected. The Church must be part of what strengthens a person for this choice. Unless the Church really opens a man for this experience it conspires to deny him life itself. That is why an institution cannot aim at preventing this kind of crisis, although some churchmen have mistakenly made this their business in the course of time. They have merely betrayed the shallowness of their own faith when they have insisted that men never test the depth of their own belief. An overinstitutionalized religion identifies its own rigid structures with the object and experience of faith. Intent on holding its accidental forms together, it can easily forget that its essential mission is to supply men with a way of life. That is why some Church leaders have emphasized a species of military loyalty to the institution

instead of a living faith. They give men a static formulation for assent rather than a creative faith that confirms
them for the course of hazards that is real life.

Christ did not treat His closest followers in this fashion.
He allowed their faith to be tested in the most desperate
of circumstances. They had to face the mystery of His
separation from them with all the consequent psychological anguish and pain that must have followed His bloody
death. His mission seemed to collapse. They were left
with His promises and the strength He had built into
them through His years of friendship with them. These
men, whose hesitancies and anxieties are clearly related
in the Gospels, had to face an enormous crisis in the dark
hours after the Crucifixion. It was in this period, about
which we know so little, that they had to affirm their
faith before it was confirmed in the Resurrection.

Psychologically speaking, each man must be allowed
to experience the same kind of crisis. It is a time of
painful search in which a man must make a choice. It is
as a man faces this that he prepares himself for the con-
firmation of the effects of the Resurrection in his own
life. The choice is clear; it is the self-affirmation of Peter
and John or the self-rejection of Judas. This is a time,
as psychologist Frank Barron has put it, of the "greatest
psychological danger, in which the integrity of the self
is challenged, and in which old selves die and new selves
are born" (Frank Barron, "The Crisis in Belief," in *Creativity and Psychological Health*, Van Nostrand, Prince-
ton, 1963, p. 148).

In the continuing course of life, a man summons up
his internalized faith in a variety of psychological circumstances. He becomes aware of his faith when he is
anxious about whether, in a certain set of circumstances,
he will make it or not. There are unnumbered occasions

for this. Men can be tempted to put aside their principles when it seems so easy to profit through dishonesty. They can feel the urge to remain comfortably silent or inactive when injustice or some other wrong demands that they speak or engage their energies in Christian action. Men can sense the hungry pulses of erotic attractions that could make them unfaithful to their spouses and, at the same time, to themselves. "Am I strong enough at this moment to be faithful to what I believe is right?" This is the kind of question a man asks himself a thousand times. The answer doesn't come from an impersonal list of dos and don'ts. His strength to affirm his faith continually comes, if it comes at all, from something alive within him, from something that can be touched by the ever present Spirit. The Church's task is to confirm men's faith through its faithful and living relationship to them. It cannot accomplish this if it is excessively preoccupied with itself. It will not accomplish this if it is so weighed down with institutional concerns that it has lost touch with man himself.

The Church as an institution is called to be a witness to the faith of the Gospels. It is meant to be the sign of hope that enables men to join themselves continuously to the struggles of life in the Spirit. That is why it is so important for it to present itself as a people of God, the mystery of human relationships in which men can find the personal responses which sustain faith and hope. It is in sharing life with others in the pilgrimage of the Church that men understand the reality of their relationship with God. The institutional aspects of the Church are essential for the encouragement of men on their journey together. This is a point often forgotten by the critics who have grown so weary of rigid structures and symbols that they would destroy them all. It is also the point that is not understood by churchmen who no longer understand that the institutions of the Church are not for themselves but for the service of men.

The institutions of the Church are human necessities to symbolize the essentials of faith. They offer the setting, through appropriate symbols and rituals, in which a man is reminded of what he believes and what he can really hope for. That is why the Spirit is made available through the signs of the sacraments. Man needs precisely these kinds of human encounters of forgiveness and strengthening to express and deepen his faith. The Church must be ever ready to renew and reshape these signs so that they will always symbolize the freshness of God's fidelity to men. The institutions of the Church are meant to be instruments of its constant pastoral presence in the lives of men. In the same way, the special servants of God's people, priests and religious, cannot offer themselves as effective witnesses if they are isolated from men by forms and traditions of life which make them unavailable to men. It is a curious truth, in this regard, that the very ones charged with speaking of faith and hope have been systematically denied the experience of love. These three elements go together. It is no wonder that many priests and religious have only been able to speak of an abstract faith and hope. The institution has cut them off, out of fear, from love. That is what cuts them off from a deeper sharing in the life of the people they are meant to serve. That is also why the priesthood and religious life seem so unattractive to many today. Rectories and convents, as insulated institutions of self-contained existences, look more like deserts than oases to pilgrim men.

The Church as a people, aware of the vital and changeable forms of its presence, offers man the community in which he can live the life of the Spirit. What really counts in life, what confers a measure of peace in a difficult world, is what we do in relationship to one another. The Church is meant to encourage and contain the human relationships that are the source of the things that really last in life. These are found in human experience touched and guided by the Spirit. It is through each other that we find and increase life for each other. The Christian community is the source of our strength for the struggles of life. Faith, hope, and love are enlarged through authentic human sharing far more than through miracles or wonders, no matter how revered the shrine at which these take place. It is with each other that we learn the lessons of the resurrected life: to trust and be trusted, to hope for ourselves and for others, to love one another responsibly, and to face death confidently. It is in providing this community of belief and love that the Church is true to its mission of service. It can give itself over to building cathedrals of structures, or it can build communities of men. There is not much evidence that it can do both at the same time.

The Church must, in other words, create the climate of loving relationships that transforms the environment of the world. It is only in this climate that men, assailed and confused by lesser values, can find the things that really last. This is the most important and traditional function of the Church, to be the presence of faithful concern and love that makes it the source of hope. The forms of the Church must constantly be renewed so that they will be, in fact, at the service of the Church's function. The Church's own faith and hope are dangerously weak when it puts its forms before its function.

The Church cannot be a stern supervisor seeing that everyone performs his obligations in a properly cheerless way. It has more dynamic and exciting work to do. It has more for men than reproofs and a satchel full of penalties. It has life itself, the life of the Spirit and the community of its sharing, to offer freely to all men. Faith, hope, and love are its gifts to the world, the best gifts of all. The faithful Church does not barter with the Gospel good news; it just gives it away.

If we may think of the Church as a maturing people, it becomes clear that a full commitment to living faith is a highly important aspect of its development. As psychoanalyst Erik Erikson has noted, "the mental and emotional ability to receive and give fidelity marks the conclusion of adolescence, while adulthood begins with the ability to receive and give love and care" (*Identity: Youth and Crisis*, W. W. Norton & Company, New York, 1968, p. 265). The Church, in the process of renewal, is facing the same choice that each growing man faces. It must internalize its beliefs and lay aside the defenses which prevent it from being a truly faithful servant. It must believe in the Gospel and the men to whom it preaches it. Structures can then be seen as the instrumental symbolizations of its mission more than as ends in themselves. The Church, in other words, is moving toward the end of adolescence and to the beginning of a more adult and loving presence in the world. The Church is finding its real self, sounding the depths of its own faith, and manifesting its understanding of the things men need most in life. Faith, hope, and love are these things that last, and these are the energies of the Church's pastoral presence and the guarantee that it will last as well.

Love As Struggle Together

Man likes things whole, from the truth in court to the satisfactory solution of detective stories. Indeed, so inborn is his need to see things whole, that he will, if presented with a series of circles that have a slight gap in their periphery, tend to perceive them as closed. Man likes things finished, tied down, and squared away. He is hung up when he cannot get things this way. Nothing frustrates the average man more than the artist whose paintings are deliberately ambiguous or the movie director whose endings provide questions rather than answers.

Nothing is less finished in life than love. Nothing resists final words said about it more than the vital relationship of friends or lovers. There is no point, while the lovers live, at which the situation can be completely and securely closed. An inevitable tension accompanies loving because it challenges man, who likes things finished, to live his most important relationship in an open-ended fashion. Love is grounded in the continuing life experience of man and woman. It thrives only on faith and hope, existential elements that are dynamic rather than static in nature. Love flowers as a growing thing. Its very nature is to be a process with no earthly terminal point.

Ronald Knox, the English clergyman-author, wrote once that the English language was at its best when it described love. It always speaks of "falling" in love, an experience that demands a free and unprotected yielding of the self in response to another. Love is not a heavily convoyed passage into the life of another. It is the wondrous but perilous abandonment of one's person to the insecure gravity of human affection.

The security of lovers does not arise from patterns that are locked in like the good wishes on a greeting card. There is no immutable store of affection carefully laid away in the numbered Swiss bank accounts of the heart. The security of lovers flows from the continuing and, at times, exhausting belief in each other, in the never ending exchange of trust, and in the extraordinarily draining devotion of love. Love is hardly ensurable because its existence depends always on the presence of freedom and choice. Lovers live in the contingent environment of accidents and aging, excitement and depression, of presence and absence. It opens out on an unchartered future. Love is, as much as it is anything, a struggle together that is always seeded with new possibilities and challenges, even in old age.

Love is full of mistakes, shortcomings, and failures. It is footnoted with second-best rather than exultant first prizes. The peace and contentment that come to lovers flow from the fact that they struggle together to understand and support each other. That is why there is so much learning in love, so much gradual wisdom and, of course, so much growth and so much capacity for giving life as well.

Young people who marry have most of these lessons

ahead of them. Nothing is more touching than the commitment of young lovers to each other at a time when the real test of their love lies in the darkness ahead of them. This is compounded for them by the pressure for early marriages and the level of romantic expectation in our culture. Young people are subjected to massive urgings to get a maid or a man, to be sexually attractive, and to achieve a basic security in life through marriage. Marriage, when it is truly understood, does not offer security in life as much as it does offer opportunity for real living. All the side motivations quickly fade and lose their compelling force if man and woman are not committed to the stressful uncertainties of sharing life together.

It is unlikely that postponing marriage to a later age will solve the problem. Young people with stars in their eyes will continue to get married when they feel like it. In effect, however, we may already have entered an age where the cultural pattern of divorce and remarriage is becoming commonplace. This illustrates the amount of learning that must take place in marriage. The first marriage becomes a testing ground, disillusioning and hardening, in which the person learns what he must know about himself in order to enter into a more stable and satisfying relationship. This trial-and-error method is full of pain. It reveals as nothing else does the challenge to human personality that arises in any relationship of love.

This is a fearful kind of challenge, one that many do not care to understand. They can never seriously commit themselves to what they cannot control, nor to the surprising sacrifices which they are not willing to make. They neither want to expose their true and imperfect selves to another nor to get involved in the process of getting to know and constantly make allowance for the

humanity of another person. The trouble with love is
that faith can always be disappointed and hope can always meet with disillusionment. These experiences cut to
the very marrow of a man's bones. He may prefer to
don some psychological armor to protect himself from
these outcomes. This is a response to fear rather than to
love. This response deceptively preserves a man from
hurt while it shuts him off from life. A man unwilling
to enter into the arduous process of sharing life with
others never understands real life at all.

Lovers are on a shared journey, one that is made more
hazardous in our day and age by tremendous emotional
demands made on the relationship of man and wife.
Suburbia is in itself isolating. The age of the extended
family, when a house or a neighborhood was full of
cousins and uncles, is fast disappearing. Many people
find it hard to get to know each other well in a highly
mobile environment. A shrinking circle of stable friends
makes it difficult for husband and wife to find others
with whom they can share the strains of family life. This
narrowed interpersonal ambiance increases the demands
that husbands and wives make on each other to be the
sole source of emotional and moral support. The increasing tension of these expectations also guarantees that
husband and wife will fail each other more often. They
cannot help it since they are only human. It is vital that
they understand the source of these pressures and their
own limitations. Otherwise the effort to share life together, even when they can only do this in an imperfect
and faltering way, will be overwhelming.

Love, in many ways, is really listening to one another.
This seems very simple and yet it has built into it the
requisite basis for the continuing experience of life together. It is when husband and wife no longer listen

and, therefore, can no longer hear one another, that their communication disintegrates. It makes no difference what the subject of their disagreement or the source of their current tension is. It is the failure to listen that eats away at their relationship and turns the struggle of life together into a renewed version of the battle of the sexes.

Listening means more, of course, than hearing the words that another speaks. It signifies rather an openness to the other person, a willingness to accept and affirm the very being of the other person. It is the very thing that lovers must offer most to each other and it is the first thing they usually give up on in relation to one another. Listening is an active process, not merely a strained silence while another person is speaking. Conversation is only a small part of this. In real listening the individual senses the meaning of the other person in life, has respect and compassion for the internal feelings of the other, and tries always to be present with the other in his or her experience.

Husband and wife must work at listening to each other. They must be ready to look at rather than look away from what is painful in each other's experience. An essential aspect of successful life together is found in this readiness to enter into this sharing of experience with another person. Counterfeit versions of life's significance abound. They are ultimately empty because they do not open a person up to the true engagement of himself with the only process that is genuinely life giving. The sharp edges of love, the sharp edges of life itself, are revealed in the need always to listen in a way that helps the other to realize that you are present with him or her in life. This is one of the areas in which the authentic spirit of sacrifice means that something in the individual dies in order that he may move into a richer and deeper life. Love is never found except it is marked with the familiar cycle of death and resurrection. In real love, then, we find the human experience that reveals the Christian understanding of the life process. Love demands death but it leads on always to new life.

This is very much what occurs when two people are willing to struggle in order to stay close to each other in their movement through life. For many the effort is too great and the price seems far too high. Some kind of arrangement must be made, something that will reduce the demands of such loving commitment. These arrangements always smack of the vague politics of fixing parking tickets or of doing business with the Mafia. The arrangement allows each partner to survive in a long slow waltz of life in which they are always looking over each other's shoulders into an unmeasured distance, deaf to the music, the crowd, and to each other. Anyone who has lived very long and has looked around himself will have seen many couples who are physically together but who are existentially very far apart. Love demands that people be present to one another.

The best of a person is involved in responding to the total demand of listening. You cannot listen unless you are ready to allow painful and embarrassing feelings to come into your experience, to taste the bitter rind of self or of the other, and to feel at times the helplessness of not being able to relieve pain. This kind of dying to self is the heart of love that accompanies the other in suffering even though it cannot give adequate comfort. It is the willingness to stick with the other even when he or she seems most remote in the fastness of their own person.

It is also this attitude of listening that allows lovers to share deeply in joy and happiness with each other. This attitude of listening is a most common but indispensable part of love. If lovers cannot hear each other, they literally cannot share anything, nor join together in giving life to others. This kind of sharing usually looks quite ordinary, is not particularly exhilarating, and may have very few peak moments. There is, however, a great solid base that is strengthened by the constant willingness to move with the other in painful growth.

This kind of love is really something that men can enter only freely. A man cannot vow himself to the obedience to the needs of the other that is the essence of loving. He cannot self-assuredly promise always to be faithful in some automatic or superficially satisfying way. It is not enough to provide shelter, food, and a semblance of social life to the other. A man can never be sure that he will have the strength for this continuing journey. He must find it at each moment, even as in that moment he is unsure that he will have enough strength for the next. The miracle of love that is willing to struggle is that the individual who is fully faithful finds that he is indeed strong enough for the next moment. This is very much the process of love that is vital and generative.

Love is shot through with the traditional Christian dynamic of death and resurrection. It is remarkable that churchmen, so fond of issuing edicts and of devising laws for lovers, have failed to listen more attentively to what the lovers can tell them about life. The most important thing for the Churches in this area is not to preach but to listen to what life itself whispers to them about the very central setting for religious behavior by man and wife. This occurs in their relationship with each other. There is no other place that you can speak to people about faith, hope, and love if you have overlooked what it means for them to share life with each other. A churchman cannot talk to them about loving God or their neighbors if he has not been willing to understand the relationship of man and woman as the creative personal source of any real human spirit of reaching out to others.

This was very much what was on Teilhard de Chardin's mind when he wrote that

> the essential core of Christianity, in my view, is certainly none of the humanitarian or moral ideals so dear both to believers and unbelievers: it is to maintain and preserve "The primacy of the Personal," extend it analogically to the whole and also positively to bring the world into contact with the supreme Person.

The obvious setting for religious behavior is hardly that of following regulations or carrying out prescribed rites. Religion worthy of the name moves easily into its true home ground in human relationships. It is meant both to illumine and vitalize these because it proclaims the meaning of unalterable love. Real religion is not afraid of sex or it is hardly true to the healthy scriptural understanding of man as a vital sexual being. It understands that friendship and sharing are exhausting challenges to human beings and it offers them the freeing insight of the Gospels to strengthen them. Perhaps it is the peculiar temptation of the clergy to stay away from the flames that leap up from the fires of real life. It is only there, however, that clergymen can find man in the supreme test of his ability to respond with the kind of love that is the highest expression of Christianity. If religious leaders are charged to give rather than restrain life, they must deal with men in the central problem of learning how to love. Religion's greatest failures have always followed on their retreat from the human scene.

Religions shrink into brittle sociological and ethnic categories when they fail to understand and join themselves
in man's sacred search for love. It is in sensing the
struggle of married people to be present to each other
fully throughout life that churchmen can learn the real
meaning of community. Without some genuine comprehension of the relationship of man and woman as deeply
religious, the churchmen can only look from the outside
in uncomprehending wonder at the essential nature of
life.

It is in human relationships, particularly in those between men and women, that religion fits into life. Religion must have something to say about the meaning of
the faith that husbands and wives need in order to make
each other whole. It must make intelligible the exigencies
and accidents of life and offer support for those who
struggle to give love and life to one another.

There is, for example, a religious truth about life that
is preached in a quite diminished way by those who do
not understand love. Quite paradoxically, love gives life
and yet it is always marked with hints of death and
separation. True lovers know that "togetherness" is an
illusion as well as an impossibility. Lovers cannot always
be together and, even when together, they are confronted
with the constant mystery of their own separateness as
persons. No sharing, sexual or otherwise, is complete or
lasting enough to plumb the depths of each other's person. There is always something beyond, always something undiscovered between people who love one another.
Indeed, a certain frustration attends lovers in their most
urgent desire to descend into the depths of each other.
There is an element of dying in this that cannot be
overcome and cannot be overlooked. An understanding
of this awesome component of love is essential or people

will only mourn their incompleteness in a despairing kind of way.

It is a strange mystery that has been understood by poets and prophets. So Kahlil Gibran still speaks to men, although dead for over a generation, "Let there be spaces in your togetherness." He is getting at the truth of the ever present limitations, the constant death which even true lovers find in their life together. This truth matches, in the existential order, what the traditional message of the Christian Gospels tells man of the inescapable rhythm of existence: life facing death with a yearning that is sustained by the hope of resurrection. The message of genuine Christianity, when stripped of the accretions of the centuries, deals with the meaning of the struggle lovers share for fullness of life together. Hope has meaning and resurrection a blinding significance for lovers who have suffered the mystery of suffering and death together.

This element of separateness, of the ability to accept differences and frustrations, of the need to tolerate absence from one another, is somehow very deeply involved in life as a continuing process. It is an essential characteristic of the quiet wisdom of those who understand the nature of real love. "Any life worth living," Gardner Murphy once wrote, "becomes topheavy with absent but cherished things." So it is with lovers who must be separated for a variety of reasons in any life together. There is work and sickness and the somewhat shattered pattern of sharing that arises as the tasks of raising children and attending to the urgent questions of domestic life mount one upon the other. There is death itself as a threat to the values which lovers hold most dear. Religion can offer an understanding and a support to those who struggle to share life in the midst of so many and varied interruptions. It can reveal the meaning of faith and hope that give the inner strength to face and survive these problems. Most of all, it can point beyond for the man and woman who long for each other and so open themselves mutually to fulfillment in God Himself. It is indeed at this point with reference to the total relationship of lovers, that the Church has a most significant truth to share with mankind.

The illuminating truth of the Gospels is that real lovers can never lose the beloved. This is the worse fear that human beings can know, the one that haunts the hearts of men everywhere in the world. It is a paralyzing fear that makes men step back from noble possibilities to more crude and primitive ways of relating with one another. The vision of faith says that love is a struggle but one that can never be marked by ultimate defeat. This is the true source of hope for man and woman who commit themselves to life together. It is in this struggle that the Church must place itself at the side of men and women to show them that it understands their struggle and can give them strength as they move together into the uncertainties of the future. Religion offers man affirmation in his loving relationships. Religion comes truly to life when it has listened to the struggle of lovers, beset with the mysteries of separation and death, and placed itself at their side. This is where life is lived and where the power of the Gospels endures.

What Have We Got to Lose?

A growing person always has something to lose. To move forward, he must constantly give up something of his past. The comfortable self-centeredness of childhood must yield to the concern for others which is the sign of the adult. The independence of the single life vanishes quickly for married couples. Dying to something secure and familiar to attain a richer and fuller level of life is both challenging and frightening. It is also the most basic truth of human experience. The dying that counterpoints growth arises from the risk of changing that a man faces when he opens himself to a new stage of life. Maturity comes only to those, according to Otto Rank, who can separate themselves from the completed phases of their development. This is traumatic but absolutely necessary if a person is to move forward. Otherwise his behavior will always be marked with the residue of childish or adolescent adjustments which have not been fully put aside.

The Church faces this kind of challenge at the present time. The Spirit guarantees continued growth but the Church must take the risk of changing itself if it is to find the fullness of its adult presence in the world. The Church has something to lose, something of the past adjustments which offered security and comfort but which are no longer appropriate. What the Church has to lose is accidental, not essential, to its nature. Nonetheless, many churchmen who are unwilling to open themselves to the next stage of renewal seem quite afraid of what will happen to the Church if it seriously takes the risk of transforming itself in order to become more fully itself in relationship to the world. They persist in defensive behavior because it preserves an illusion of security and exempts the Church from the challenge of growth. That is why they are so fond of speaking of the "unchanging Church." Defensive behavior delays the trauma of growth but it destroys its promise at the same time. Defensive churchmen fear the loss that is inevitable with development far more than they exhibit faith in the Church's mission to maturity. They refuse new responsibilities in favor of holding on to old certainties. They deny the future because they are more comfortable with the past.

The growing individual feels uneasy about taking a new step in life because he thereby surrenders a position which is both familiar and rewarding to him. Growth makes him anxious because he will be different if he commits himself to it. Settling on an achieved plateau of growth appeals to him even if this adjustment does not challenge the best that is in him. He may fear the new learning which continual development requires of him. He knows the territory that surrounds him quite well but the map of the future is uncharted. A step forward means that he will allow new influences into his life, new relationships and new responsibilities toward himself and toward others. The stable ground of his present adjustment is soothingly familiar to him and it is painful to leave it behind. That is why so many men hold on to a childish self-centeredness long after they have reached adult age. It is difficult to give up the view that the world centers on and serves them. So too, some people find that the secondary gains of illness, such as attention and sympathy, are so rewarding that they are quite reluctant to accept the strength and independence of restored health. They limp through life hypochondriacally because they do not want to lose the responses from others which sickness gets for them. Every man, sooner or later, must fashion his own answer to the question "Are you willing to pay the price of growth?"

This same question presents itself now to the Church. It is clearly the nature of the Church to grow to splendid fullness. To share itself with all men it must give itself trustingly to the process and pain of growth. This process and pain constitute the human elements which are the sign and seal of the action of the Spirit, the source of the Church's life. The Spirit does not operate on impersonal structures; the Spirit breathes into the human beings who are the Church. These persons are in turn responsible for the vitality of the Church in relationship to all men. It is their business to see that the forms of the Church are adequate to its function. It is up to them to modify and renew structures so that the Church can continue to grow and accomplish its mission of service to the world. Frightened men, afraid to lose something of the past, cannot respond to the Spirit and so they resist the development of new forms which can express the Church's servant role ever more creatively. It is difficult to understand what churchmen really have to lose if they understand the nature of their stewardship. They do not preside over a rigid bureaucracy, although they cling to the defenses which make it seem so. Their responsibility is far greater. They are meant to foster the growth of the living organism which is God's people.

What do hesitant churchmen seem to be afraid of? They are reluctant to give up familiar, if ineffective, stances of relationship because these have become quite comfortable over the years. They do not know what a renewed institution would look like, and so it is with great caution that they contemplate modifications in the present structures. They feel the anxiety that comes from facing new tasks of learning and adjustment. These churchmen equate tradition with truth. They only theoretically accept the fact that, although truth never changes, its understanding and expression do. It is safer to stick with formulations from the past than to do the serious thinking that is required to translate the meaning of the Gospels according to the new understandings of human experience and scholarship.

They are afraid of allowing new processes to take over because these will be so markedly different from the past. A stubborn insistence on the monarchical model of the Church makes it difficult for them to implement the collegial approach in a wholehearted way. The repeated cry that "the Church is not a democracy" is the defensive gasp of men who are truly frightened at the prospect of introducing democratic and pluralistic procedures in the life of the Church. The commitment required to do this unsettles their long-time reliance on authoritarian relationships. The threat of yielding up some measure of power is very real to them. They fear, in other words, the loss of the brittle security that outmoded structures seem still to offer them. Yet the heart of the Gospel message demands an open and loving rather than a manipulative and controlling Church. Defenseless love demands growth, and men with an affection for power know exactly what they will lose if they assent to this.

What would be lost in the practical order? A few examples suggest the secondary gains that are preserved when institutional reform is not wholeheartedly endorsed. The first thing that hesitant churchmen seem to fear that they will lose is the faithful. Over and over again they have uttered phrases about the need to avoid scandalizing members of the Church through processes of change which are too rapid. "Easy does it," as a distinguished archbishop said to me. The evidence, as a matter of fact, seems to run just the other way. The People of God are strong in faith. They are confused by changes only when they are not openly and thoroughly educated for them. Everywhere people are looking for the Church to respond to their needs more effectively. They want the Church to function in relationship to them and they are more scandalized by the conflicts generated by dying authoritarianism than by almost anything else. People want a Church which understands them as persons, has a feeling for their needs, and helps them to achieve the Christian values of faith and hope and love in their own lives. It is impossible to imagine how a Church which makes itself more capable of service could cause any disaffection among the faithful. This occurs only when the Church does not serve them. This is precisely the situation when forms from the past break down and cripple the Church's function of ministry.

Some churchmen suffer a more concrete fear about the loss of financial support which renewal might bring about. As one harried pastor told me with great feeling, "Keep changing the Church and there goes your dollar bill!" And God knows that the dollar bill was important in the heavily mortgaged age of building the parish plants of America. Only the most unrealistic would think of subsisting on manna from the skies, but a Church that places service to its people first need never worry about money. An earlier period demanded a lot of it to raise the structures to house and educate the Catholic people. One of the signs of the times for the Church is the ending of the muscular phase of building churches, schools, and convents. We are in an era where the faithful are no less generous but where their needs have changed. Oddly enough, this is so because of the success of the period which provided the opportunities of education for the generation now come of age. They look now for the Church's sensitivity to their deep personal needs for community, participation in the mission of Christianity, and a heightened sense of relationship to God. These things are not built by hands. There are no blueprints for them except in the Gospels. Churchmen who respond freely and generously to these needs understand that changes must take place in the model of typical Catholic life. If people experience the Church in closer relationship to them, they will not fail to take care of its material needs. It is doubtful, however, that Catholics will continue to contribute without a better understanding of and voice in the way their money is spent. This truth also dictates structural changes in the Church. The people know too much about the frozen wealth of the Vatican treasures and the multiplying interest on its stock portfolio ever to be unquestioning contributors again.

Some churchmen feel that the loss of religious personnel is somehow attributable to the transformations of renewal. If anything, the loss of priests and religious is the evidence of the breakdown of old forms within the Church. The losses and the lack of vocations at the

present time point to the need for a radical rethinking
of the structures of the priesthood and religious life.
This is necessary not for the convenience of individuals
but for the life of the Church. Personnel leave its service
not because the Church has been changed but because it
has been so little changed.

A barely conscious fear of many of those in authority
in the Church arises from the prospect of losing control
over people. There is no doubt that the forces of renewal
have loosened the far-ranging control which Churchmen
came to exercise over the personal and public lives of
so many Catholics. Renewal challenges them to rediscover the positive qualities of leadership and to put
aside the magisterial model of minutely regulating the
lives of others. What they will actually lose if they
endorse the renewal of Church structures is the enormous
and aching burden of unnecessary supervision of the life
of their people.

The key to this, of course, is their ready acceptance
of collegiality as the structural dynamic of the age. They
must wholeheartedly engage the Christian people in active responsibility for the Church's mission of service in
this world. This will take monumental patience and a
great willingness to trust people but it will also guarantee the vitality of the Church and the effectiveness
of their own leadership. Wider participation on the part
of individuals is clearly one of the demanded characteristics of all institutional renewal at this period in history.
The election of bishops is one example of this. There
is no guarantee that democratic elections will improve
the quality of the hierarchy. It will, however, engage
the energies of the people in a respectful way in the life
of the Church. This will give them a new sense of trusted
participation in the Church and a deepened sense of

loyalty to its leaders and its mission. It is when people do not experience an active sense of participation that they become estranged from any organization. As Allport has expressed it:

> When the ego is not effectively engaged, the individual becomes reactive. He lives a life of ugly protest, finding outlets in complaints, strikes and above all in scapegoating. In this condition he is ripe prey for a demagogue whose whole purpose is to focus and exploit the aggressive outbursts of nonparticipating egos. ("The Psychology of Participation," in *Personality and Social Encounter*, p. 193)

The greatest risk for the Church, then, is to fail to trust its people and to leave them as passive and increasingly restive outsiders. They are indeed prey to the extremist elements which batten on their disaffection. A great deal is irretrievably lost for the Church and the world when this occurs. The authentic renewal of Church structures not only prevents this but guarantees a healthier presence of the People of God as witnesses together of the Gospel message.

There is surely the danger that the relationship of the Church to other spheres of life, such as the political and economic, might be radically altered by renewal. Positions of political influence and economic security might truly be threatened if the Church were to surrender some of its long-held beachheads in these areas. Tax exemption, the condescension of commerce and industry, the whole establishment kinship; all these might be very different if the Church committed itself fully to the recovery of its Gospel identity. In other words, the very powerful position of the Church which arises because of prestige and political influence could be lost if the Church exchanged dominion for service. It seems so difficult to disengage the Church from the social class affiliations which have developed over the centuries. Yet it has developed these by allowing itself in many ways to be reduced to living in the "religious" dimension of human affairs. Sociologically, it has accepted this role and its perquisites at the danger of losing its vocation. A loss of power in order to rediscover a sense of mission seems like a mighty risk to those who seriously believe that the Church's influence depends solely on its investments or on its acceptance by what is known as the establishment. All these alliances would be in possible jeopardy if the Church takes another look at its real function in the world.

This does not mean, of course, that the Church's function would necessarily alienate it from the major moving influences in society. If anything, it would be committed to serve them in a responsible way. This, however, would demand a revitalized attitude of Christian concern which would break the lock-step identification of the Church with these elements.

What the Church would really lose if it committed itself to this kind of change is irrelevance, the sad burden of being blocked off in a very narrow and pseudoreligious enclave of life. The Church, in other words, that moves toward being a true witness to the world can no longer be manipulated or controlled by the political or economic forces of the world. Its spiritual message is no longer diluted through fear of losing its worldly security. If it preaches the Gospel to men, the powers of the world will find the Church painfully relevant to all the real problems of this age. These powers can retaliate on a massive scale at institutions bold enough to disturb their collective conscience. There is great loss possible here, a crucifixion and death for the servant Church which might make it cry in anguish: "Now my soul is troubled. And what shall I say? Father, save me from this hour! No, this is why I came to this hour" (John 12:27). It is this kind of death which the Church must be willing to endure if it is to live its redemptive life of service to mankind. The Church serves men, not the powers which manipulate men. Its redemptive vocation has always demanded that the Church be a suffering servant.

There are, however, secondary gains to irrelevance which are difficult to give up. The world still gives respect to churchmen, especially when they mind what has been called "their own business." That means holding worship services, performing other strictly religious rites, and being a supportive but cooperative ecclesiastical presence in the affairs of men. Inaugural prayers and invocations clearly belong in this realm of behavior. These are rewarded but that does not make them vital expressions of a servant Church. Something different occurs when churchmen take positions on peace, race relations, and personal values in a technological age. Indeed, these questions are the Church's business when it perceives clearly its role of ministry to human need. It is, in fact, called to confront society with Christian values but this automatically removes it from the safe and acceptable sidelines of life. The achievement of relevance may lead to the loss of ready acceptance by those segments of society which would be disturbed by this activity. Boat rockers are always in danger of being thrown overboard.

To speak out for man demands that the Church constantly run the risk of being disliked by those who are dismayed by the message of Christ. Churchmen never enjoy being disliked by anyone. The Church cannot be true to itself unless it is willing to run this risk. This is its first obligation just as much as it is the first obligation of every person.

It is interesting to note the characteristic changes of an individual who is searching himself in therapy for his real identity. To pursue the analogy of the Church's struggle for fullness as similar to that of the person in counseling reveals the same dynamics of self-discovery and growth. The individual moves away, first of all, from façades of behavior, from the masks of adjustment which hide rather than reveal the true self. He moves, as Carl Rogers has noted, "hesitantly and fearfully, Houghton Mifflin, Boston, 1961, p. 167). So the Church, in the process of renewal, has been inching away from the ill-fitting façades of monarchy and bureaucracy, away, in other words, from what it really is not.

The person who is growing also overcomes the compulsions of behaving according to expectations from outside himself. He begins to sense his internal identity and to act in accord with it. In the same way, he gives up merely trying to please others, because this causes him to be artificial instead of genuine. This same dynamic is clearly evident in the renewing Church which is grasping more firmly its own nature as a people called to proclaim the Gospels and to serve others in accord with this understanding.

The individual becomes more self-directive and less dependent on the cues given to him from the outside. He becomes more responsible for himself, for his own complex and growing personality. He gives up wanting to hide things from himself and from others. The resultant openness puts him in a more vital relationship to himself and to all other men. He can accept and trust himself and he can accept and trust others as well. His relationships improve as he becomes more authentic. His real qualities are a sounder basis of relationship than his defenses ever were. What he has grown to become is far more valuable and rewarding than the defenses he has lost in the process.

This is very much what is taking place in the Church as it finds itself again in relationship to men. When it is genuine it is much more effective in serving others than when it operates from behind defenses. The Church reaches men more truly and they respond to it more genuinely as it becomes its real self. The Church discovers that it is safe to reveal itself as a searcher, complex and imperfect in so many accidental ways, because it is now true to itself. What it had to lose is nothing in comparison to what it has gained and what it can now give to other men. All it really loses is a sense of conflict and pain, the discomfort of wearing masks that it was never supposed to wear in the first place. The risk of change, of dying to the self, is worth taking because nothing else opens the Church to being fully itself for the sake of the world.

The sacrifice of image for real identity is the redemptive core of the process of institutional renewal. In truth, the Church has nothing to lose but the chains which have bound it defensively in the past. It can then present itself unadorned and defenseless as the servant of the world. This is its vocation and the vision of its real promise as a saving presence for mankind. Those who resist the renewal of the Church are fighting the very forces that guarantee the fulfillment of its true nature. They only retard the growth that the Spirit would give it. There is, in the long run, nothing that can be lost if the Church takes the risk of becoming itself again.

The Now and Future Church

Along with the rest of mankind, the Church has entered the age of curiosity about the next century. "Futurology" has become a national pastime, the sign of man's ever present urge to pull aside the curtains of fate and to locate the DEW line of history. Seers, however, often suffer from the Cassandra complex. It is tempting to develop a sympathy for the abyss.

There is also the danger that we can succumb to the pull of contemporary culture and take all of our cues about the future from it. This is not to say that we should ignore modernist culture. It is, however, to remind us that the model of the future Church is still found in the Gospels. There is a message, of course, in the prophecies that are so clearly present in the cultural spokesmen of our day. Poets and artists typify the open and sensitive men who can feel the shifting of culture under their feet before the rest of mankind. They hear the singing in the rails long before the express train of the future rounds the bend and comes into the present. They are viscerally attuned to these changes and they try to tell us about them in their writing and works of art. Because they sense changes before other men, the problem they experience in one generation is frequently the problem that all men must face in the succeeding generation.

Had we listened to the poets and artists earlier in the century we would not now be so puzzled by the challenge to institutional forms which has become such a compelling problem for all mankind. A generation ago this was the problem with which the artist was already engaged. He was trying new techniques and testing new materials to see if they would bear the weight of the human experience he was attempting to describe. The Church should hardly be surprised at the present challenge to its institutional forms, especially because of its traditional definition as an *ecclesia semper reformanda*. The Church, in other words, always seeks to find the right form of expression for its work in this world.

If we listen to the poets and artists of today we find men speaking about the future who have been served less than well by the Church itself. They do not have the vision of the meaning of life, which the Church should have supplied to them in language that they could understand. Their prophecies are pessimistic. These cannot serve as the prediction of the Church's own future, although they do tell something about the problems to which the Church must respond if it is to speak to this age.

Modernist culture, according to Irving Howe, runs the double risk of being too subjective and of standing passive in the face of irreversible fate. The cry becomes "I see, therefore I am" in a world dominated by the perceiver. This is indeed the trend when institutions fail to renew themselves, fail to reform their presence in the world. There arises the tendency to a subjectivity which is divorced from or, at best, marginally related to, the real world. In this situation men build and inhabit worlds of their own. Their dominant mode of adjustment becomes narcissistic. They are unable to postpone gratification in a cosmos that begins and ends in themselves. Relationship and responsibility for relationship to others is set aside, a sense of community is lost, and alienation becomes the slogan of life. This tendency fits into the view of the increasingly sensate society which has already been unveiled as a possible environment in the post-industrial world.

This is also, unfortunately, the condition of many prophets in the Church whose vision has been diminished not only because of their own shortsightedness but because of the failure of the Church to deal effectively with the problem of institutional reform. Since the Church does not speak to them they listen to the soundings of their culture. They hear the prophetic echoes of men who have not been nourished by the hope of the Resurrection.

Beyond subjectivity is the modernists' pervading sense of the "historical impasse," of man, as Irving Howe puts it, mired "in the hopelessness of a life without anterior intention or terminal value." There seems to be no way out, "no exit," as Sartre has phrased it. These are the perils for ecclesiastical prophets today: to view everything solely from their own point of view, and to despair at even the possibility of a solution. These are dangerously self-pitying visions, even though they hold up to man the mirror of his journey when it is uninformed by the good news of the Gospels. These are the visions of the future that come to man when the Church has not taken seriously its tasks of presenting itself in modern form to mankind.

But the Church is called to have visions and to dream dreams, to give hope to a world which has lost its way and which now seems to be stumbling toward doomsday. That is why it is important not to misread the questioning of structural forms which is so widespread in the Church. This is an urgent task, not simply so that the Church can share the same style as the culture around it, but so that it can accomplish its main task of serving the culture which it is meant to transform. Those who resist institutional reform in the Church are, in the long run, resisting the Church's dynamic inner nature and thwarting its ministry to the world. When the Church is not able to relate itself effectively to the world, there is nothing left but the mournful voices of men who sense the blackness of an unredeemed universe.

The process of turmoil which we now witness in the Church is a sign of hope. The Church has begun the process of reordering itself to be true to its calling, to re-form itself. Because of the vitality in the People of God and their eager response to Gospel values whenever they are truly presented to them, not only the Church but the whole world can have hope. The Church is re-discovering its orientation toward what is new, toward a future full of hope through the proclamation of the Gospel and its generous service to man. By trying to make the Church secure, renewal-resistant churchmen take hope away not only from the members of the Church but from the world, which desperately needs the view of reality that Christ entrusted to the Church so that it might share it with all men.

I have often tried to compare the Church with an individual person in psychotherapy who is seeking his own identity. The then Cardinal Montini, in the first session of Vatican II, described the work of the council in terms of the Church's search for its true identity in relationship to mankind. Indeed, the new definition of the Church as a People suggests that the analogies derived from the understanding of the human person can be very helpful.

A therapist must be a prophet of sorts. At least he must have some sense of prognosis about those who come to him. He assesses their strengths and weaknesses. So must we if we are to establish some estimate of the outcome of the process of search for its true self which the Church initiated in the Second Vatican Council.

What is a person like when he comes to therapy? He hurts in some way. That does not mean that he wants to change himself. It doesn't even mean that he is ready to recognize his own hurt or to admit his own feelings and meanings as really belonging to himself. The way he views the world is often extremely rigid. He is, in the phrase of psychologist Eugene Gendlin, "structure bound." He interprets present experience in terms of what he has known in the past. He cannot fully sense the meaning of what is happening to him in the present. Close and communicative relationships are frequently looked on as quite dangerous. The person at this stage does not recognize his problems and has a tendency to communicate about externals. It is not he who has the problems. They are all in the world around him.

It is not difficult to apply these descriptions to the way the Church found itself at the beginning of Vatican II. It was hurting but it was unable to identify its hurt or to admit much about its own feelings of confusion and conflict. The Church was indeed extremely rigid in the way it viewed the world. It had constructed its own self-contained universe and tended to view other religions and movements in highly stereotyped fashion. It was, in a classic sense, "structure bound," unable to face the present except in terms of the past. It could not open itself fully to present experience nor modify itself in accord with it. The pre-Vatican II Church clearly regarded close and communicative relationships as dangerous. Love between persons constituted a very difficult situation for the Church to understand. It tolerated love but it was not at all comfortable with it. It was all right in the abstract but quite painful in the individual concrete case. I recall a major religious superior who once said to me, with some concern about my writings, "How can you love *some*body when you are supposed to love *every*body?"

It was difficult for the Church to admit that it had any problems at all. What problems there were existed in the world around it, in the wiles of conspirators who were always trying to overturn its foundations, in the plots of willful men who were the enemies of the cross and of Christianity. If this slightly paranoid style of adjustment were not enough, there was always the tendency to deal with life in terms of externals. This has been documented sufficiently through the life experience of all those who survived the golden age of canon law.

What is hopeful at the present is that this mode of adjustment has become dislodged. It no longer works very well. Even when the Church did not admit problems, it found that its behavior got it into conflicts and difficulties a good deal of the time. It tended to isolate itself from the affairs of mankind. This became so extreme that it could be tolerated no longer. In other words, this smug and closed-off style of adjustment to the world finally broke down. The Spirit broke it down through the Second Vatican Council. Even though this process is still in its preliminary stages, solid hope springs from the fact that it has in fact begun.

We can expect defensiveness from a person with this kind of adjustment, a shying-away from looking at all the aspects of his life. In therapy, however, the doctor cannot allow the patient to choose what he will look at or he may become a part of the patient's defense mechanisms. So modern Christians do not allow the Church to be selective about what it will study in itself. They demand that it look at everything. If this makes the defenses more obvious, it also increases the chances of their crumbling.

André Malraux wrote in his *Anti-Memoirs* that "the truth about man lies first and foremost in what he hides." This may well apply to the Church and the defenses with which it chose to hide its true self over the centuries. We have already discussed some of these in an earlier chapter. Intellectualization, for example, allowed the Church to talk about things without doing too much about them. Denial made it possible for the Church to say that there was no problem. Dissociation allowed the development of good theory even though this was often divorced from effective practice. Projection permitted the authorities of the Church to blame others for any difficulties that might arise. "You are the disobedient ones," they could say, and thus shield themselves from any deep self-examination. One hardly needs to go further in reviewing all-too-familiar stances on the part of the defensive Church.

What a person talks about a good deal in the beginning of therapy is usually not the central problem at all. So it has been with the Church, where the central problem is not celibacy, birth control, or even authority. It might be noted that these are, in the minds of authoritarian churchmen, always the problems of others, a projection out from the Church into the body of the faithful. It is, in a certain sense, easy to talk about these things. Beneath these concerns, however, lies the prime problem of whether a person, and in this case the Church, can get in touch with his real self. The question is whether he can reintegrate himself through finding again the meaning of growth. It was from growth as a dynamic process rather than a static condition that the Church has become estranged. Somewhere it lost its feeling for life. The present challenge, as it is for the person in psychotherapy, centers on whether it can come alive again. If the individual is challenged to give himself over to life through the process of self-search, the same challenge presents itself to the Church. The underlying problem that puts all others into perspective is summed up in asking whether the Church can stand to grow or not.

It is the Church's vocation to be a source of life. "I have come that they may have life and have it to the full" (John 10:10). The Church is meant to understand and promote growth. It can only do this if it is unafraid to experience it. The Church must, through the action of the Spirit, enlarge the lives of others. Behind all the talk, this is the essential problem, the solution of which determines whether the Church has a future or not. It can grow into the future but it cannot back defensively into it.

The struggle of the person in therapy at this stage can be very disordering. He experiences many hostile and negative feelings. Indeed, these may dominate at this time. It is painful to give up what he has been hiding in order to find the truth about himself. No therapist has witnessed this kind of struggle without sensing the quality of newness which attends the person's discovery of his real personality. Many have described it as something like the act of creation because the individual is bringing his real potential into being. This is characteristic of growth, something that has been noticed by parents and lovers throughout the ages. This leads to a person's fresh understanding of what he is really like. He no longer needs to say defensively, "I know everything." As he opens himself to further learning and growth, he can now say, "This is all I have been able to understand so far."

He changes, in other words, in relationship to himself. Because of this he changes in his understanding and relationship to reality and to others. He assumes a new responsibility for himself, for the fullness of his best self, as well as a new responsibility for others. He can grow and he can allow others to grow.

This catches very much the quality of newness that is so essential to the Church that seeks always to reform itself. It is indeed "a new creation." A Church is clearly growing when it no longer needs to say that it knows everything. It can say, in great truth and hope, "This is all I have been able to understand so far." The Church is breaking away from the so-called "religious" dimension of culture to which it had confined itself for such a long time. It is capable now of growing and of allowing others to grow. It is this quality of newness, this freshness, which makes it a source of life for all men. It can now offer its real self, quite undefended, to the world around it.

It is this drive for newness that characterizes the process with which the Church now finds itself engaged. It is looking for hard truths but it is still very defensive. The Church will have to tolerate disorganization if it is to achieve a new and continuously renewing self. It has a long way to go before it discovers its full identity and senses that growth is a process of continuous change rather than a successful securing of various bastions of existence. It is worthwhile to note that the achievement of identity is a task of adolescence. The achievement of identity is only the beginning, in a sense, of a person's relationship in a mature way to others. So too it is with the Church. The discovery of its identity, which will make it look different to those who knew it before, will signal only the beginning of a more adult relationship with the world.

A new Church is now, in fact, building, one that rises in response to the breath of the Spirit. It is a Church with a quickened sense of the Gospel commitment to the future, one that is not "structure bound" to the past, nor to the artful embalming of tradition. This is a Christianity which is ending its schism with the world as it reaches for its identity as rooted in the "Testament of the New." As Moltmann has described it:

> We are confronted here with an eschatologically oriented faith. It is not concerned with an event that took place at the beginning of time nor with explaining why the world exists and why it is as it is. It is oriented to a new future, and hence its object is to change the world rather than explain it, to alter human existence rather than elucidating it. The eschatological attitude toward the world is concerned more with making history than with interpreting nature. (Page 12) Jürgen Moltmann in *The Future As The Presence of Shared Hope*. Edited by Maryellen Muckenhirn, Sheed & Ward, 1968, p. 12.

If the process of growth in the Church is to continue, we must be ready to grow through opening ourselves to the Spirit of growth. We must then be ready to face the consequences of the changes that will be worked in us because we have lowered our defenses. These changes will indeed make us look different, because we are different, to those who once looked upon us. The future of the Church arises from our willingness to give ourselves to the present, to understand the struggle of God's people to grow and to commit ourselves to that struggle.

This new Church, which has already manifested its vitality in many ways, will look different because the accidentals, which have been so persistently misidentified with the essence of the Church, will be transformed and will no longer be the subject of our total concern. The Church will look different because the processes that are already under way are irreversible. Sooner or later people will realize that these changes are signs of a healthy reorganization rather than a disintegration.

The Christian community is reforming itself in the present, calling the Church again into being through taking responsibility for preaching the Gospel. The Gospel is only preached, according to Romano Guardini, by those who realize that authority is service and power is love. The movement of the Church into the future does not take place separate from our affirmation of and our commitment to it under the guidance of the Spirit. Across the world there are Christians who are responding to this vision of the Church that has become again the servant of mankind. These people give themselves to the future because they have rediscovered in the present the eternal newness of the Gospels. They constitute the source of strength which means that the process of growth for the Church will continue. They understand that their anointing by the Spirit bids them to be the Church for the future.

No Christian can doubt the availability of the Spirit, particularly at a point in history when all human institutions are confronted with the challenge of self-renewal. The Church, if anything, should provide a model of restructuring to the rest of society. The strength of the Church lies in its people, sufficient numbers of whom have given evidence of their ability to respond to the Spirit's invitation to grow. This is the source of vitality which can free the Church from the paralysis of time-worn structures and can guarantee the development of effective future structures. These people have heard the call which summons them to be the Church for the sake of the world at this time. They are ready to serve mankind and to give themselves away in response to its needs.

These people are not the eccentrics but the solid core of Christians who have rediscovered their priesthood and the varying gifts of the Spirit which enable them to exercise it. They understand the social heart of Christian life and the need the Church has for a recognizable communitarian presence. Their energy and their capacity to share the Christian life with others is immense. One need not be a poet, or much of a prophet, to sense that these people are already here and that their presence assures the Church of a future. Sometimes a person in psychotherapy fails to sense his own strength, and consequently he never even tries to use it. He is mistrustful of his real personality and so he never brings it into life. This is exactly the position in which the Church now finds itself, strong enough for new life and ready for the future, and yet not quite prepared to face and employ its real strength. This is the challenge for ecclesiastical

leaders today: to commit themselves to leading forth
the people who give the Church a future.

These growing Christians have sensed the profound
truth that there is only one essential aspect of the Church's
relationship to the world: ministry to it. As Hans Kung
has observed (*The Church,* Sheed & Ward, New York,
1967, p. 485), this ministry "means the renunciation of
dominion over the world, the renunciation of power politics, of the claim to secular leadership, secular prestige,
privileges and distinctions." They have the distinctly
Christian gifts to share with mankind. The first of these
arises through knowing what the world is about. "The
Church has the gift and responsibility of seeing and
understanding the world as it really is: with understanding and openness, with criticism and freedom, with gen-
erosity and charity" (*Ibid.*).

Indeed, as Kung goes on to specify the general dimensions of the ministry of the Church to the world,
he lists the very vital hopes of Christians everywhere:
to be linked to the world, to be committed to the world
in pro-existence rather than coexistence, to fulfill its vocation of being a witness to the world. These describe
the function of the Church. From a solid grasp of this,
many new and different forms of service can and must
be developed both for individuals and the community.
The forms will flow from a wholehearted embrace of the
perennial function of ministry in undefended service to
mankind.

Those with the problem are the ones who misread
the signs of the times and continue to resist growth as
they hide behind their defenses. There are many in this
group, some of them in places of authority, and it is
a problem which they themselves must solve. Spinoza re-
minds us that "what Paul says about Peter tells us

more about Paul than about Peter." So too what these men and women say of the Church, whose future eludes them because they do not understand its present, tells us more about themselves than it does about the Church. Many leaders in the Church show too little commitment to growth and to life. They resist new forms because they do not understand the Church's function. It must be emphasized again that these are the ones with the problem. They will, because of the increasing pressure of events, finally be forced to face their own defenses, put them aside, and reintegrate themselves into the Christian community. Sooner or later, these leaders will have to ask questions about their own identity. They will have to ponder the root meaning of *authority* as signifying "to make able to grow." They will have to listen and hear the Spirit speaking to them through the Christian community which is already eagerly pressing forward with the reassurance that God who has begun a good work in them will see it through to completion.

One could predict many accidental features of the future of the Church and seem Delphic indeed. Most of these predictions could describe the accidental features that will take the place of the Catholic cultural forms which are now passing away. This, however, would miss the central understanding which Christians must attain of our own implication in the growth process of the Church, the pains of which are jolting but reassuring. The Church is not a cold and lifeless planet spinning like the moon only because of the pull of the earth, that other and distant world. The Church is not a satellite of the secular world. It comes alive in relationship to it and gives it a vision of its meaning and destiny that is unavailable if the Church does not speak. The

Church is called to save the world, a minority, as Kung puts it, always serving a majority.

Christians who sense the call of the Spirit can see a future that is kept from the eyes of the poets and artists of contemporary culture. Those who do understand the eternal newness of the Church constitute "a company of anti-nothing," as Ernest Bloch says, "who on the basis of their hope refuse to abandon the world to evil, inhumanity and the powers of destruction, since they remain true to the utopian dream of complete salvation." All Christians help the Church to grow when they themselves grow. Each of them can say, "For this was I born and for this did I come into the world."

At the end of his book *The Church* Hans Kung asks the question, "Has the Church a future?" His answer is important for the People of God who are stirring to the challenge of growth and who understand that institutional change must follow from this impulse of the Spirit. It is also important for those in authority who have not yet solved their own problem about a Church which has rediscovered its newness and its commitment to man's future. Kung says:

> The reply to this must be: The Church has a future because it has a present in the world . . . the Church has a future because in the darkness of time God's grace is given to it, giving it a present full of light . . . the Church has a future because through God's grace it was given a beginning, which in the present is a promise and a hope for the future. Indeed, the Church has a future; it has *the* future. (*The Church*, page 489)

Indeed the Church has *the* future because it possesses the Gospels whose power to change men's lives remains undiminished. The Gospels and the future are too exciting and challenging for a man to commit himself to them in a lukewarm or defensive way. The Gospels remain the liveliest words around because they are the words that give life. But the Gospel life is granted only to those who are willing to die for it. A lot of people do not like the idea, much less the reality of crucifixion in their own lives. Nothing of real value lasts very long for those who will not see or understand this core truth of redemptive living. Man will not really secure his future with armaments and treaties, with the blind alley politics that tolerate little wars and big bombs to preserve peace. He will find the future when he finds again the meaning of his life, and this is precisely the gift that the Church has for the human race. It cannot give it if it remains defensive; it will not give it unless it suffers death to the outmoded forms whose burden has sapped it of so much vitality. A resurrected Church arises even now, a People of God with fresh faith and hope and love for the human family that has been waiting to hear the Good News for a long time.